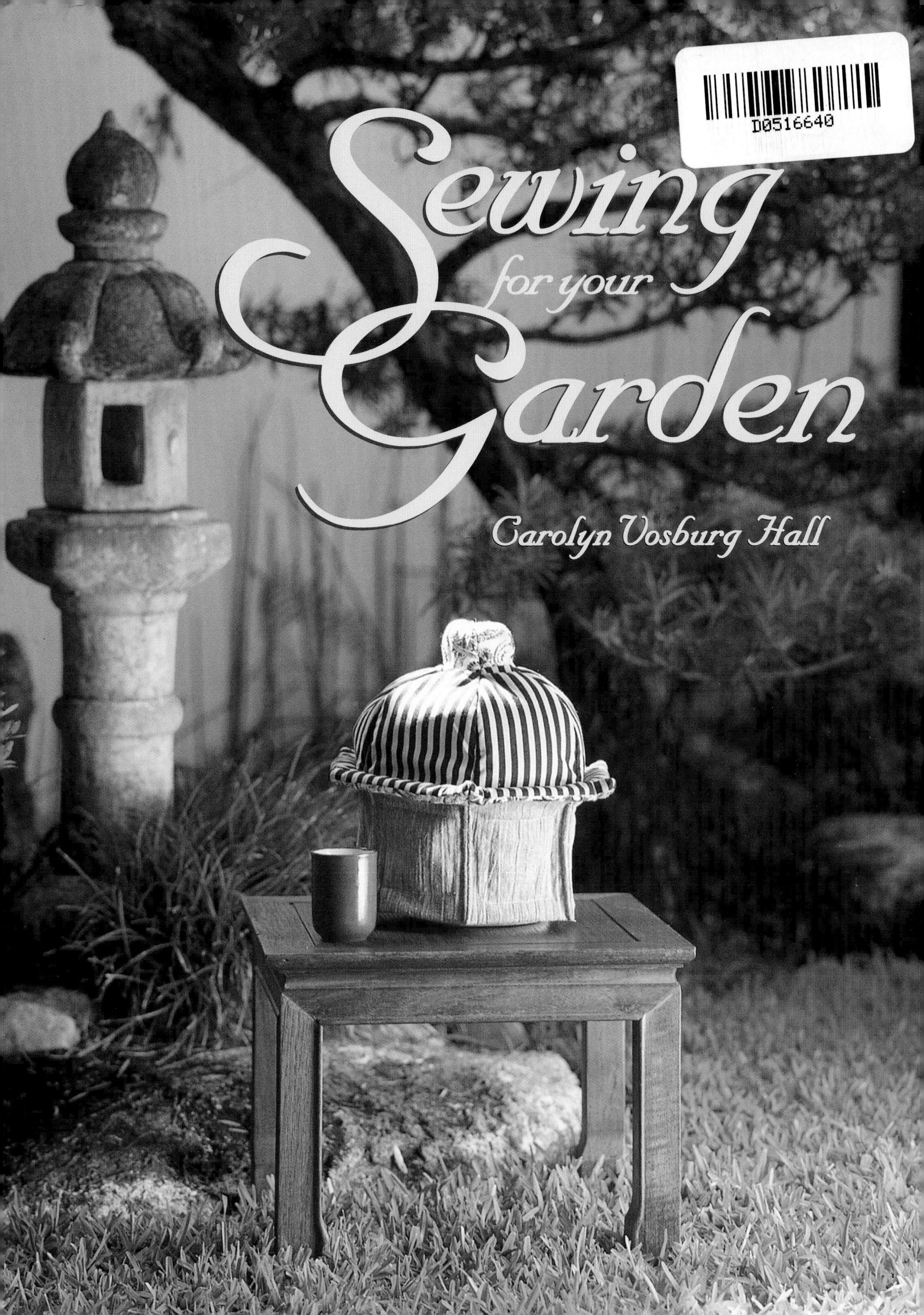

Sewing for your Garden

Carolyn Vosburg Hall

krause publications
700 East State Street, Iola, WI 54990-0001

Please call or write for our free catalog of publications. Our toll-free number to place an order or obtain a free catalog is 800-258-0929 or please use our regular business telephone 715-445-2214 for editorial comment and further information.

Some product names in this book are registered trademarks of their respective companies:
Bernina® 1630/Bernette 334D
Pacesetter by Brother® PC 7000
Elmer's® Glue
HeatnBond®
HTC Craft and Quilting Needle-punched Fleece™
Polarfleece®
Minwax Polyacrylic®
Berol®/Eagle Prismacolor
Singer® Genie
Sulky Threads®
Sunbrella®
Thermal Fleece™
Velcro® Brand

Photography by Carolyn Vosburg Hall, unless otherwise noted
All drawings and project designs by Carolyn Vosburg Hall, unless otherwise noted
Book design by Jan Wojtech
Manufactured in the United States of America

Library of Congress Cataloging-In-Publication Data

Vosburg Hall, Carolyn
Sewing for your garden
1. title 2. sewing 3. outdoor crafts

ISBN 0-87341-670-8
CIP 98-87372

Cover photo by Carolyn Vosburg Hall
Title page photo by Jane Letchworth

Acknowledgments

Thanks to Jane Letchworth and Claudia Hall Stroud for photographic assistance, Barbara Gash for editorial advice, Hattie Stroud for project ideas, Leslie Masters for banners, and thanks to my wonderful editor, Amy Tincher-Durik.

Thanks, especially for lovingly-tended garden settings and models for photographs, to Doug and Claudia Stroud, Hattie and Bradley Stroud, Rand and Pat Hall and kids—Briana, Brent, and Ross—Al and Phyllis Zacherlie, Carol Chadwick, Garrett and Joan Hall, Don and Audrey Busse, Wallace and Jane Letchworth, and the provider of my garden and studio, Cap Hall.

Your garden spaces can be "exterior decorated" like Carol Chadwick's Victorian-style pergola, or in a variety of other styles shown throughout the book.

Foreword

From "down and dirty" garden weeding, to light and pretty patio entertaining, you'll find in this book a wealth of information on projects to make for the great outdoors. The limitless imagination of author Carolyn Hall has once again surfaced to produce fresh and clever ideas for enriching our lives.

The book is carefully thought out and organized in logical order. Hall presents each theme separately, enticing us into the mood with her descriptive introductory paragraph. This is followed by step-by-step directions for making various items that suit the occasion. As a bonus many of these creative techniques can easily adapt to other projects we might sew at another time.

Carolyn Hall's personal enthusiasm is felt throughout the book. Her writing is light and easy-going, always honest, often humorous. The accompanying diagrams, drawings, and photographs help make this book even more user-friendly, and best of all, great fun!

Barbara Gash
Detroit Free Press Sewing Columnist

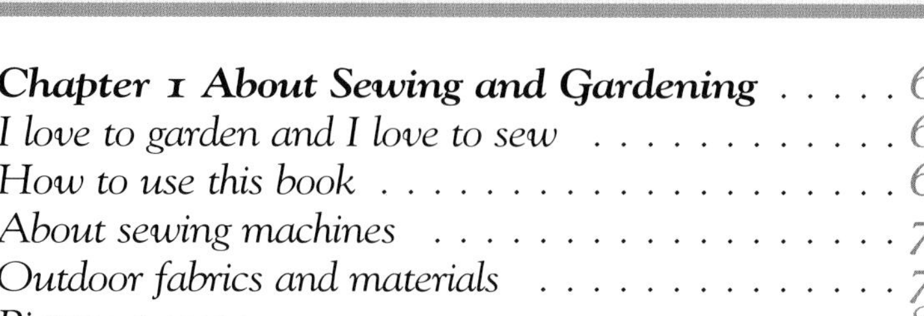

Table of Contents

Chapter 1

About Sewing and Gardening

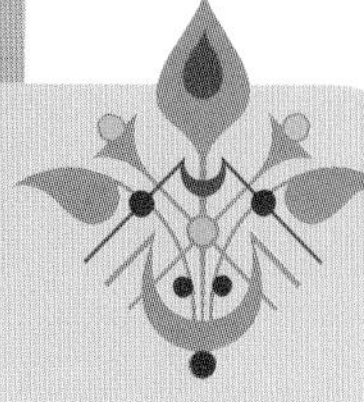

I love to garden and I love to sew

Gardening means much more than toiling in the soil. It includes all kinds of outdoor living in casual space. What stitcher doesn't want to furnish and decorate that space?

The greatest pleasure with both sewing and gardening is anticipation, envisioning things to come from your planning and creating. No need for boredom when your mind bubbles with visions of projects to sew or things to plant. And what pleasure comes from tools in hand cutting, marking, weaving strands together. (Laugh if you will, but in my garden I braid spent daffodil leaves and coil them under the burgeoning hosta leaves to mature as they require.) For many of us both sewing and gardening dovetail nicely. When weary of sewing, take your clippers and snip off the deadhead flowers in the garden. When the sun shines enticingly, take a hand-sewing project outside to enjoy the day.

How did the idea for this book come about? Easy. I love to garden and I love to sew. I like to bring plants inside to nourish the winter months and make visual rooms outside. Both sewing and gardening delight the senses. Think of the wonderful combinations of colors both flowers and fabrics provide. Imagine how your hands enjoy the feel of fabrics from soft to crisp and how your fingers itch for the moist spring earth and fragile new plants. Do you, too, like the sounds of the sewing machine whirring industriously, the shovel clinking on a stone in the loam, or the birds singing and children playing as you work? Some smells please the nose such as gentle peony blooms or new fabric, while some smells offend, like molding leaves or fabrics full of chemicals. You know you are alive.

How to use this book

This book offers fabric projects that you can create to use outside as well as inside. Included are 50 designs for tablecloths and totes, sun hats and wind socks, tea-cozies and sand bags, blankets and apron knee pads, among others. These projects can help you dig in your garden, serve lunch on your patio, frolic by the pool, picnic on the grass, barbecue a treat for dinner, tailgate at the Big Game, or celebrate the 4th of July.

Projects range from very-easy-to-make to complicated-but-worth-the-effort. None are as big as circus tents. I thought about designing big stuff, like tents, umbrellas, or hammocks, but decided to include objects of more manageable magnitude. If you are sometimes sorry when a

project is completed because the doing of it is more than half the fun, try the patchwork tablecloth, the Heron wall hanging, or the fish floor cloth. For fast projects try the fireworks napkins, the circle tablecloth, or the coasters.

All of the projects list the fabrics, supplies, and tools needed to create them. Photos and diagrams show how. None take long to make even if you have only short bits of working time. Read the instructions first because some methods or techniques may be new to you. Some information is boxed with the project, for example, squaring fabric or sewing synthetics. Some shortcuts to save space are used; for example, "Repeat" means to do the same step(s) over for the second piece.

Most of the patterns are based on geometric shapes, mainly rectangles and circles, so you can measure and draw them with a yardstick and carpenter's square directly on paper or fabric to scale up to size. Patterns are shown on a grid to assist you in doing this. The few complex shapes are given full-size so you can photocopy or trace them.

About sewing machines

Because all objects are sewn by sewing machine or serger, only changes from ordinary sewing are mentioned such as using a leather or ballpoint needle, setting the machine for free-motion stitching, or using the differential feed on the serger. Alternative ways to accomplish the same results are given. Read your sewing machine manual for help.

Common sewing machines were used to make these objects: my old Singer portable and my new Bernina. Less common is the Brother PC 7000 computer machine for embroidery. The serger, a domestic version of commercial machines, not only sews but overcasts and trims seams all at once—plus no bobbin winding because thread comes continuously from big cones.

With a regular machine you can pin at right angles to the seam and remove the pins as you come to them or sew carefully over them. Serger manuals say "Don't pin baste" with good cause. Hitting a pin will break the serger blade and may throw the timing off. If you must, pin parallel to the seam more than 1 inch from the **left** side of the cutter, and never right of the seam line (this gets clipped off) or any future seam line (too easy to lose track of pins).

"We could never live anywhere without a garden," author Carolyn Hall says. "Here at our new condo our plants moved in before the furniture."

Outdoor fabrics and materials

Like summer days and lily blooms, nothing lasts forever. Fabrics used outdoors must be tough to withstand sun fading, rain, mildew, other eroding factors, neighbor kids, and ourselves. Yet, the trend is to ever more outdoor living from portable plastic chairs to stylish cast aluminum furniture, from brick to tile patio floors, from awnings to pergolas overhead. And with this comes the same affection for beautiful fabrics like those used indoors.

Both indoor and outdoor fabrics are used through-

On Don and Audrey Busse's lanai, fabrics are used in many ways: sewn with gathering and welting for a plant pot cover, soft-sculptured into pillows, glued on a table top, and painted on a canvas floorcloth, among others.

out this book. These include: Sunbrella, a 100 percent acrylic in a tough, tight weave made to resist sun and rain—a good choice for totes, hats, cushions, and, of course, umbrellas and awnings. Another has a vinyl coating adhered to a fabric backing which is lightweight and waterproof for rain coats, totes, or tablecloths. Polyester canvas is more water resistant than cotton canvas; both are tough. Resin-coated stuffing fibers make draining wet cushions easier. Nylon flag fabrics resist fading, don't sag when wet, and glow colorfully with back lighting.

Many indoor fabrics go outside as well, including upholstery, chintz, organdy, and lace. Best to bring them in after use, but you can let them take their chances with the weather. Sheer voile flows gracefully in the breeze. Brocades and metallics brighten any scene. Fabrics can be chosen for many reasons: color, texture, strength, wear, ease of handling, cost, availability, and more. Experimentation is fun.

Picture a scene...

Wonder what color to use, what kind of fabrics? Picture a scene showing whom the project is for and how it will be used. This makes design decisions easier. The people in this book's photos are real, my friends, my children, and my grandchildren. I designed projects for their special outdoor places and color-coordinated each scene especially for them.

For example, Florida friends Phyllis and Al Zacherlie's lifestyle epitomizes indoor/outdoor living. Their house opens into a screened lanai full of plants, fossilized shells, and patio furniture. The screen door opens to the yard full of plants and trees cloistering sitting areas that frame views of the drawbridge over the bay. It's my ideal, the way they live with plants in and out—even their pets come in and out, including a wounded pelican who comes for a daily handout. For Phyllis, a filmy cover-up seemed right for entertaining, topped with a sun hat straight out of a medieval fair, and a tablecloth for one of her several garden tables.

To create your own scenes you can switch colors, change fabrics, or combine patterns or any other details. And if it's a good day you can even sew outside. Use your patio table to lay out fabrics, use the brighter outdoor-light for better vision on fine sewing, and use the fresh air to cheer your spirits.

OPPOSITE: Phyllis Zacherlie, in a voile and lace cover-up, entertains on her patio in Sarasota, Florida. The Zacherlie's parties are legendary! Leslie Masters painted the organdy banner.

Chapter 2

Sewing for Your Garden

Photographed in Claudia and Doug Stroud's Garden

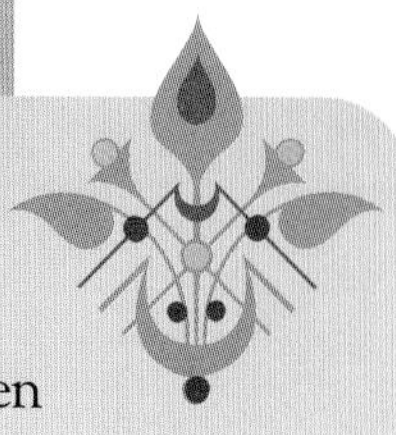

Shown in Claudia and Doug Stroud's garden are useful items you can easily sew: a denim work jacket, sun hat, knee-pad apron, weed bag, and embellished gloves. They all make great gifts.

Gardeners wear a certain amount of dirt around, a weed pulled here or an earth smoothed there, so why not dress for it. These first patterns aim to solve some gardening problems: how to carry tools in your pockets, keep knee pads in place for kneeling, shade your eyes, keep your hands clean, and tote weeds and clippings without dragging the trash can around. This first project is a cheerful denim jacket that you can make in the colors given, or in plain old blue denim, if you prefer.

Square your fabric

Cut pattern pieces from squared fabric. Patterns include an arrow for placing them on-grain because off-grain cut pieces shift askew. To square woven fabric the easiest way, tear it straight across. This may pull threads and leave a "furry" edge. To avoid this, pull a thread across and trim on this line. If the resulting corners aren't square, pull in opposite corners to square. Some exceptions exist, such as a geometric design printed off-grain or if an applied surface prevents this.

The piece of denim for the garden jacket shown would not square by tearing across, pulling a thread, stretching corners, or steam ironing. So I threw it in the washer and dryer to put it back the way it was woven. Once out of the dryer it was even more angled! So I accepted the fact that this twill-woven fabric was forever askew, but at least stabilized. I laid it flat on my measuring grid, used a carpenter's square to square it, and laid the pattern pieces on-grain to the warp threads.

Don't panic. Most fabric behaves very well. You may need to wash your fabric first to stabilize it.

Project 1:

Work jacket

Denim makes a cool-weather jacket and protects you from brambles and bugs. The jacket is loosely fitted and can be made by anyone with average sewing experience. This makes a medium-sized jacket. For a different size, add or subtract your dimensions when drawing the pattern.

You need:

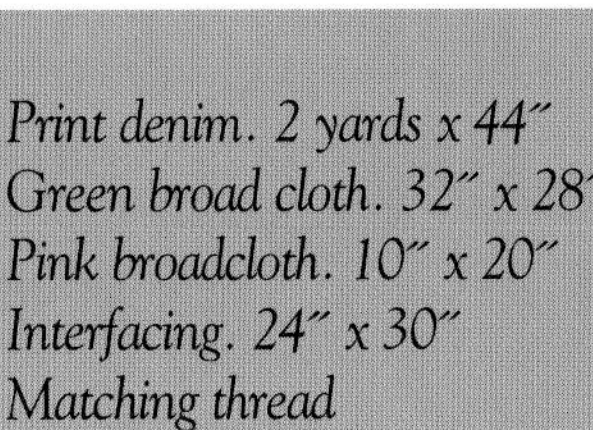

Print denim. 2 yards x 44″
Green broad cloth. 32″ x 28″
Pink broadcloth. 10″ x 20″
Interfacing. 24″ x 30″
Matching thread

4 green and 2 yellow 1″ buttons
Tools: scissors or rotary cutter, leather or heavy-duty sewing machine needle, yardstick, pencil, pattern paper

PATTERN: Photocopy to size or draw the pattern adjusted by your measurements.
PATTERN PIECES: A front (cut two, one reversed), B back (cut one on fold), C collar (cut one pink, one green, one interfacing), D sleeve (cut two), E pocket (cut two denim, two green), F facings (cut two green, two interfacing), G small pocket (cut one pink, one denim), H neck facing, I pouch.
Cut out all pieces. Seam allowances 5/8″.

SEWING THE JACKET:

1 Serge or overcast the edges on pieces A, B, D, F, H, and I as shown.

2 Sew the pockets, the collar, and the pouch.

A. Align the collar pieces face-to-face, plus the interfacing. Sew the edges, leaving the bottom open. Clip the corners, turn, and press. Mark the center.

B. Match pockets E and G with linings. Seam the edges, leaving the bottom open. Clip the corners and turn. Tuck in the raw edges 3/4″ and press. On the right

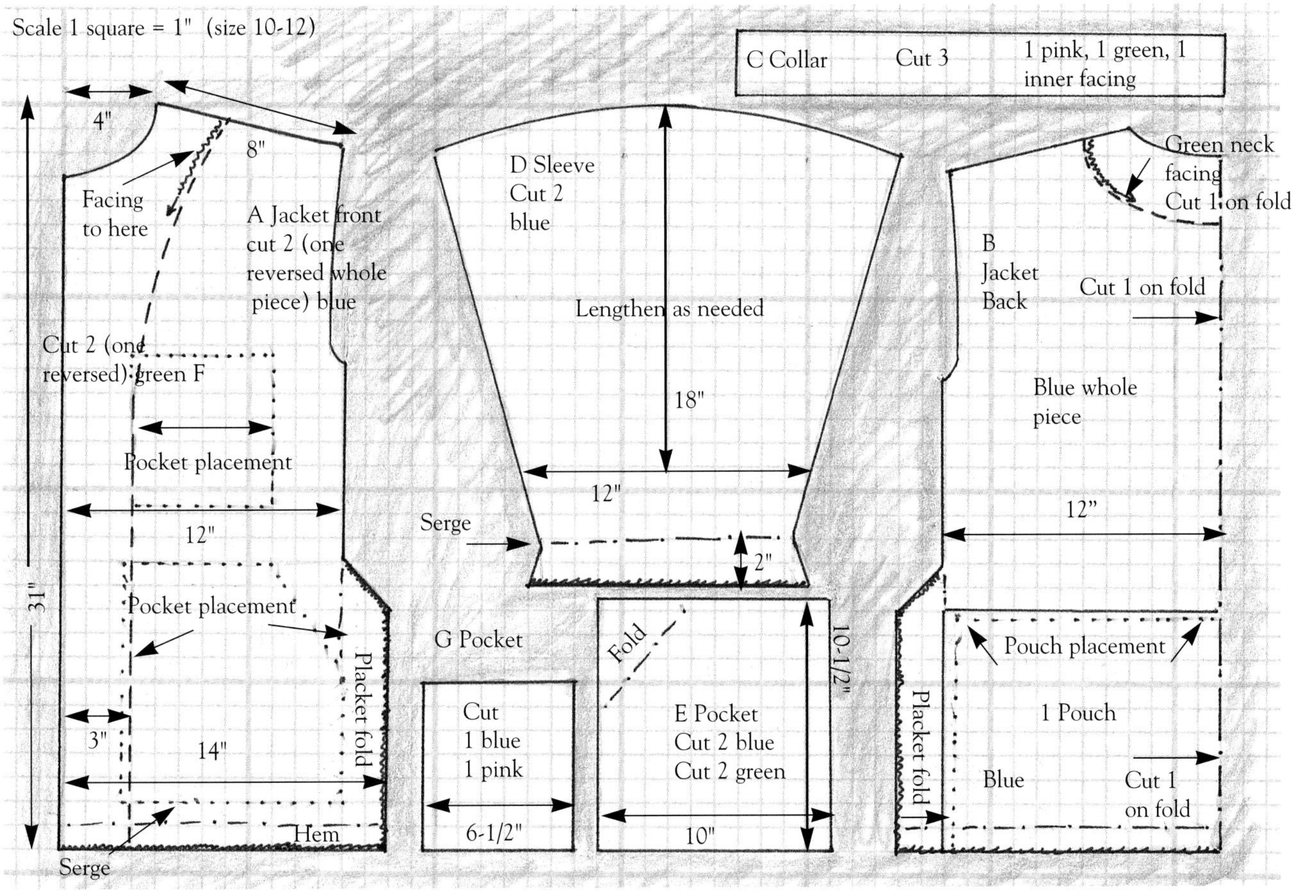

Scale 1 square = 1" (size 10-12)

C Collar | Cut 3 | 1 pink, 1 green, 1 inner facing

4" | 8" | Facing to here | A Jacket front cut 2 (one reversed whole piece) blue | Cut 2 (one reversed) green F | Pocket placement | 12" | Pocket placement | Placket fold | 3" | 14" | Hem | Serge | 31"

D Sleeve Cut 2 blue | Lengthen as needed | 18" | 12" | Serge | 2"

G Pocket | Cut 1 blue 1 pink | 6-1/2"

Fold | E Pocket Cut 2 blue Cut 2 green | 10" | 10-1/2"

Green neck facing Cut 1 on fold | B Jacket Back | Cut 1 on fold | Blue whole piece | 12" | Placket fold | Pouch placement | 1 Pouch | Blue | Cut 1 on fold

OPPOSITE: Claudia Hall Stroud wears a denim work jacket with lots of pockets, including a skinny trowel slot and a back pouch.

pocket E topstitch in 3/8″ from the edge across the top to 4-1/2″ down the right side. Mark a vertical stitch line 4-1/4″ from the right edge. On the left pocket topstitch in 3/8″, across the top to 4-1/2″ down the left side. On the small pocket topstitch in 3/8″ from the edge across the top.

C. Assemble the pouch pieces. Hem the ends and press a hem across the top edge.

3 Mark the pocket placements on the fronts A and back B. Place both pockets E on the front, 2″ up from the bottom, 2″ from the center front, and aligned with the side. Topstitch to join around the pocket except where the pocket is already topstitched. Repeat for the other pocket E. Align the small pocket 2-1/4″ up from pocket E and 3″ from the center edge. Topstitch the vertical line in the right pocket to make a trowel pocket.

4 Prepare the front.

A. Match the facing F face-to-face with the inner edge on front A and stitch from the bottom to the neck. Press open, fold back, and press.

B. Fold the side placket face-to-face with the front A. Measure up 1″ (the width of the hem) and stitch across the facing and the placket at this point. Clip the seam allowances and turn both corners.

C. Press the hem. Topstitch across the hem, placket, and facing.

5 Prepare the back.

A. Align the pouch faceup on the back, bottom edges matching, and serge or overcast across.

B. Fold the side plackets face-to-face with the back B. Measure up 1″ (the width of the hem) and stitch across. Clip seam and turn. Iron a 1″ hem in the jacket back, including the pouch.

C. Flip the pouch up, pin the hemmed top edge to the back, and topstitch the hem.

6 Align the fronts to the back, face-to-face at the shoulder, and stitch. Align the facings' top ends to the neck facing ends face-to-face and sew.

7 Pin the collar to the jacket neck, matching the centers and front edges. Baste this joining. Align the facings and collar/jacket face-to-face, pin, and sew. Clip or grade seam allowances, turn right-side-out. Topstitch in 3/8″ up the right front, around the collar, and down the left front.

8 Match the sleeve top center with the shoulder seam line face-to-face. Fit it to the armhole, pin, and sew. Repeat for the other sleeve. Align the sleeve and jacket sides and pin at the arm seams. Sew from the sleeve end to the top of the placket, 10″ up from the hem. You'll need to unfold the placket a bit for this seam. Bartack the seam ending. Double-fold a 1-1/2″ hem on the sleeve, or as needed, and topstitch.

9 Sew buttonholes and buttons as marked or use Velcro patches or snaps. Fold down the pocket flaps and sew on a button.

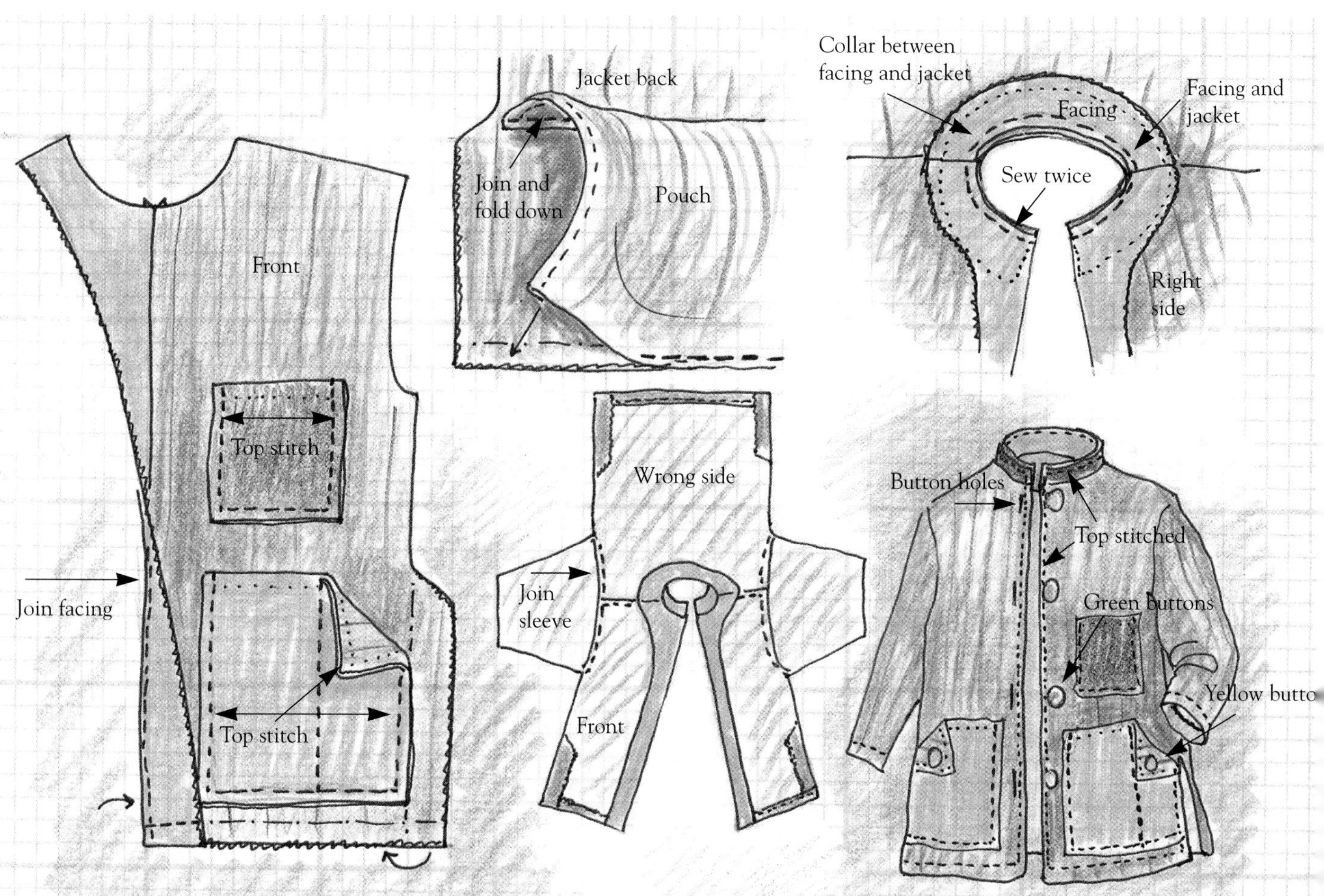

Project 2:

Weed tote

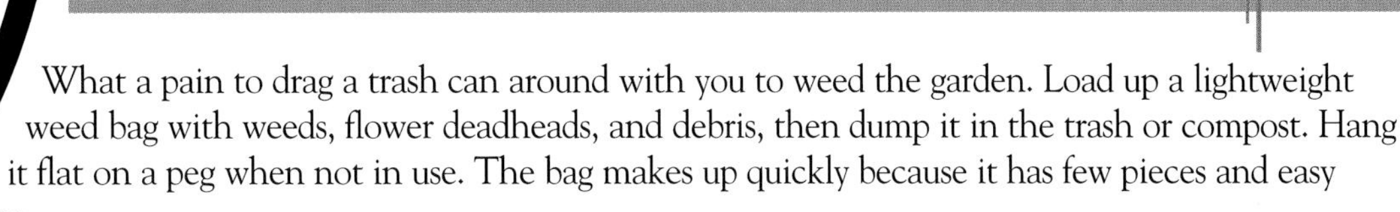

What a pain to drag a trash can around with you to weed the garden. Load up a lightweight weed bag with weeds, flower deadheads, and debris, then dump it in the trash or compost. Hang it flat on a peg when not in use. The bag makes up quickly because it has few pieces and easy seams.

This canvas weed bag holds unwieldy trimmings, totes them to the trash can, and then stores flat.

FABRIC: I used heavy-weight water repellent cotton canvas, which is washable. "Who washes a weed bag?" my neighbor asked. So, make a lightweight vinyl-coated fabric bag and hose it off, if you prefer.

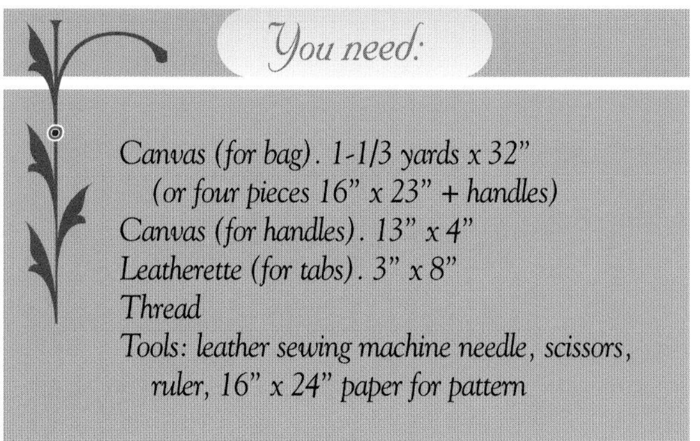
You need:

Canvas (for bag). 1-1/3 yards x 32"
(or four pieces 16" x 23" + handles)
Canvas (for handles). 13" x 4"
Leatherette (for tabs). 3" x 8"
Thread
Tools: leather sewing machine needle, scissors, ruler, 16" x 24" paper for pattern

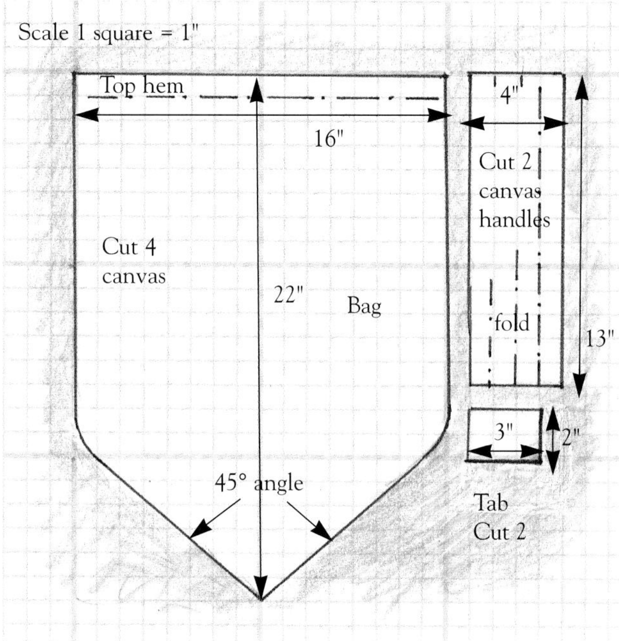

PATTERN: Scale up or photocopy the diagram to size. Bag side (cut four pieces), handle (cut two strips 4″ x 13″ canvas), tabs (cut four 3″ x 2″ brown leather, plastic, or canvas).

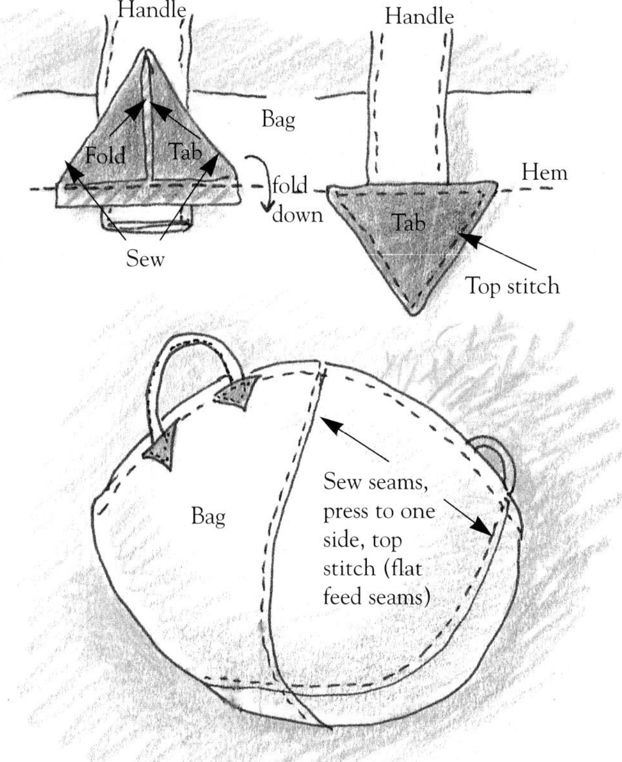

Making the bag:

1. Match two sides face-to-face and serge or overcast from top to tip. Fold to one side and topstitch this seam. Join the other two sides.
2. Match the joined sides face-to-face and serge or sew from top to top.
3. Fold a double 1″ hem in the bag top edge. Topstitch in 1/4″ on both hem edges.
4. Handle: Fold edges to the center, fold to cover raw edges, and topstitch both edges.
5. Pin the handles on opposite bag sides, centered 5″ apart, overlapping the hem 1-1/2″ from the top. Topstitch.
6. Place a 2″ tab on the handle end face-to-face, with the bag overlapping the hem's lower seam. Sew across the seam line. Fold the tab corners to the center to form a triangle. Fold in or trim off the top edge corners. Topstitch the triangle in place.

Project 3:

Knee-pad apron

Knee pads are useful, but I hate them. The straps bind or the pads slip. So here's an apron pattern created with built-in knee pads and loose straps to keep them in place. It looks a bit like gaucho pants or cowboy chaps, which is logical because it was designed for protection, too.

Vinyl and similar fabrics are a bit difficult to sew because they stick to the presser foot and needle plate. There are several things you can do to ease this: Use a Teflon-coated presser foot and foot plate. Stop sewing often to lift the presser foot to ease puckers. Use tear-away backing. Or hold the fabric firmly while sewing before and behind the stitching to guide it through (without pulling so hard as to skip stitches).

LEFT: Pop on this protective waterproof apron for a quick go at the garden.

BELOW: Separate knee pads always bind or slip, but these sewn into the apron do not.

You need:

Vinyl-coated flannel or canvas + knee pad fabric.
1 yard x 42″
1″ wide Elastic. 24″
Thread
Tools: leather needle, scissors, pattern paper, pins

Fabric: I found this great vinyl-coated stuff on the remnant table. It has a fluffy flannel backing, comes 56″ wide, is very flexible, and does not ravel. For a hot day, make an apron of lightweight poly-cotton and the knee pads of canvas or leather. Add more padding in the knees as needed.

PATTERN: Scale up or photocopy the pattern to size. For other sizes, measure across the hips 5″ below the waist to clothing side seams. Measure from the waist to the knee for the apron length, add 6″ for the knee pads, and 6″ more for doubling the knee pads.
Apron sides (cut two, one reversed), pocket (cut two, one reversed), belt (cut a strip 2″ x 72″; piece if necessary).

Making the apron:

1 Apron side: Turn a 1/4″ hem along the pocket edge and topstitch. **Note:** the vinyl does not fray. For a woven fabric turn a narrow double hem.

2 Fold the knee pad up 6″ back-to-back and topstitch the top edge.

3 Align the pocket faceup under the side faceup and pin in place. Topstitch a double row along the curved edge.

4 Fold a hem 1/2″ wide on the side outside edge. Slide the elastic into the hem at the bottom edge and pin. Hem the side from waist to bottom including the elastic in this seam. Topstitch the elastic to hold. Align the elastic across the leg, fold the 1/2″ hem in the inside edge, tuck the elastic into the hem, topstitch the elastic three times to secure, and sew the inside edge hem up to the center seam.

5 Repeat steps 1 to 4 for the other side. Align the sides face-to-face and join from the waist down 12″.

6 Waist: Sew long stitches across the apron top and pull the thread to gather slightly for a better fit. Match the tie strip at the apron center face-to-face and pin. Sew the tie to the apron with a 1/2″ seam allowance. Fold the tie strip over the seam allowance, pin, and topstitch in the ditch along the waist to secure.

7 Ties: Clip the unfolded tie hem 1/4″ at the waist on both sides. Fold a double 1/2″ hem in the ties lengthwise and topstitch.

Options: Add more padding in the knee pads if you wish. Sew on a layer of leather, heavier vinyl, or other fabric to reinforce the knee pads. Add another knee pad layer if these wear out.

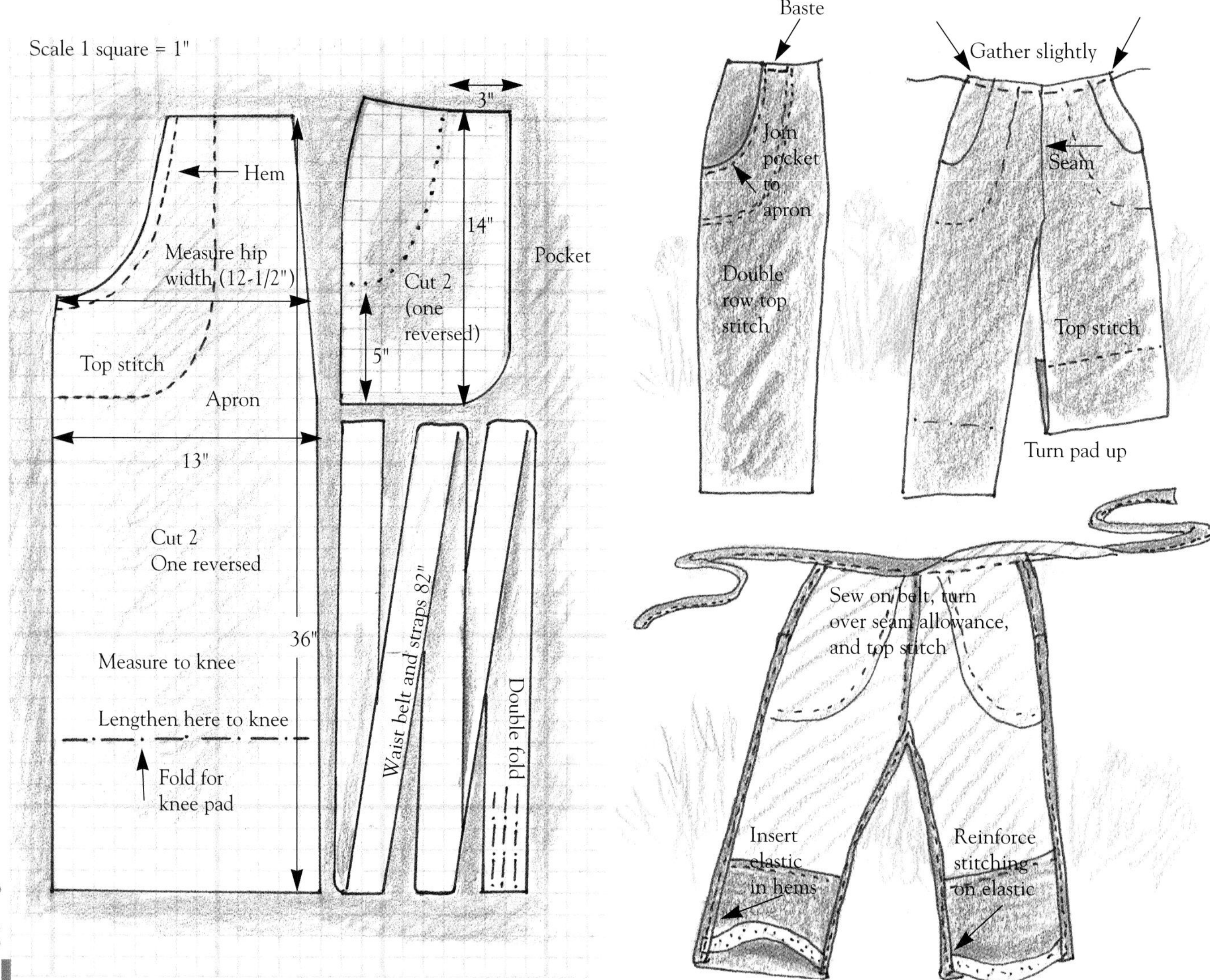

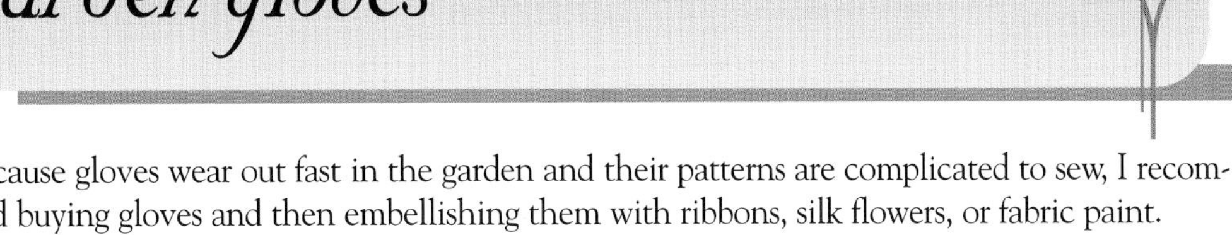

Project 4:

Garden gloves

Because gloves wear out fast in the garden and their patterns are complicated to sew, I recommend buying gloves and then embellishing them with ribbons, silk flowers, or fabric paint. Decorate the ready-made gloves to cheer your weeding along or give as a gift.

The purple glove flowers are wired onto a safety pin and tied with a ribbon for a pin-on "wrist corsage." The other flowers are tied around the glove with a ribbon for easy removal.

TO DECORATE GLOVES YOU NEED: Garden gloves, pliers with clipper blades, scissors, silk flowers, florist's wire or plant twist-ties, safety pins, and ribbons.

Test your arrangement with one, two, or three flowers, cross the stems, add leaves, and bunch in ribbon. Don't make this corsage wider than the glove. Clip off the wire flower stems. Wrap the wire or twist-tie around the flower stems tightly and include the safety pin. Tie the ribbon around the bundle tightly and tie a bow, or wire the flowers and leaves together, tie the ribbon around the glove wrist (loosely), and tie the flowers in place with a ribbon bow.

ABOVE: *If anything can make weeding fun, these embellished gloves can!*

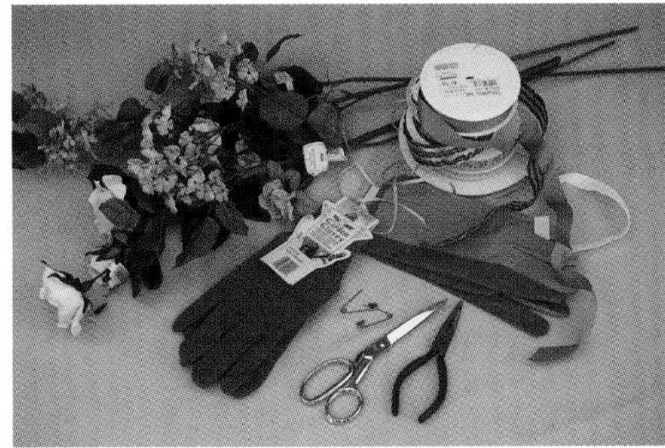

Collect supplies and tools for trim, including needle-nose pliers, florist's wire or twist-ties, pins, ribbons, and silk flowers.

Clip off wire flower stems, form the "corsage," and wire them to a safety pin. Tie a ribbon around the wires, pin, and tie a bow in front.

Decorate ready-made garden gloves with flowers, ribbons, buttons, or paint.

Project 5:

Hat

Here's an easy washable hat to wear in the garden. Use denim, poly-cotton, or scraps from your fabric stash to make this. Use colorful gingham, poly-cotton, or whatever suits.

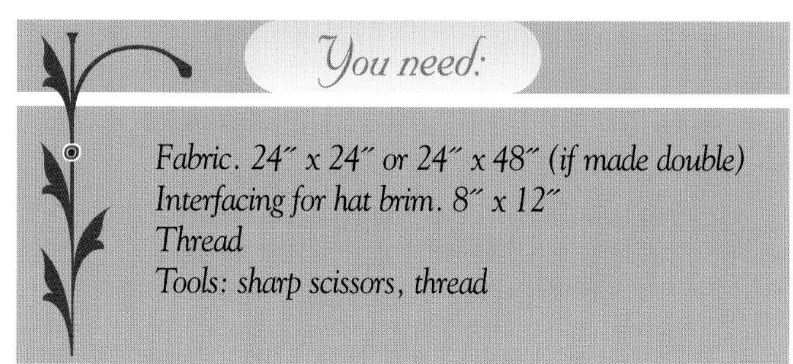

Fabric. 24″ x 24″ or 24″ x 48″ (if made double)
Interfacing for hat brim. 8″ x 12″
Thread
Tools: sharp scissors, thread

PATTERN: Make a paper pattern according to the drawing. Cut one crown (or two for lining), three bills (one canvas, one lining, one interfacing).

Fold a narrow hem (or serge) all around the crown edge except for the center 14″. Sew a gathering thread across the front edge and gather to 13″. Stack the bills face-to-face, plus interfacing, seam the outside edge, trim to 1/4″ seam allowance, turn, and press. Align the bill with the gathered front of the crown, pin, and sew. Fold the seam onto the crown and topstitch.

For a lined crown, match the crown and lining, sew the edges except for 14″ in the center front, and turn. Align the bill with the crown opening and pin to one side of the crown. Stitch. Fold the crown seam allowance in, align it over the seam, and topstitch.

To wear, tie the two crown "tails" together over the center ìtailî on the back of your head.

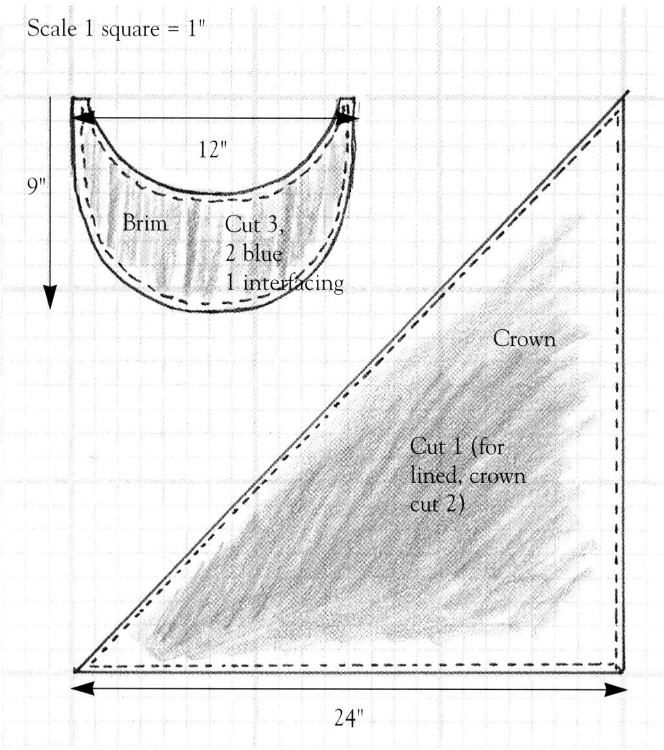

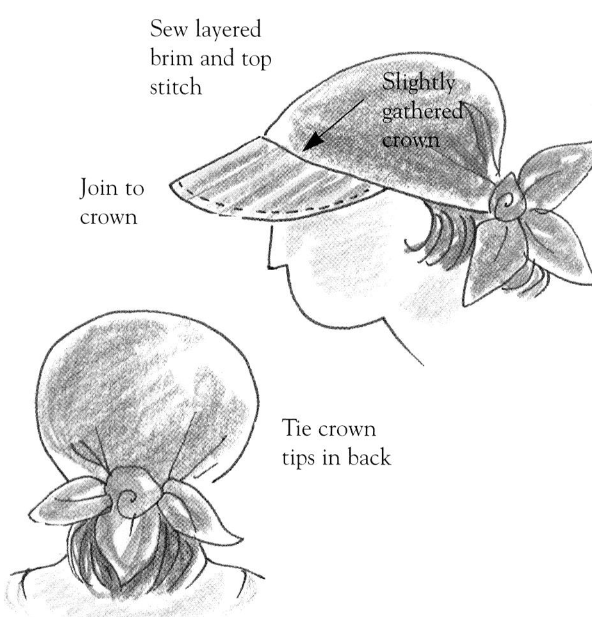

Chapter 3

Sewing for Your Deck

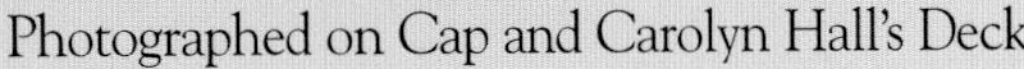

Photographed on Cap and Carolyn Hall's Deck

Nature, the out-of-doors, provides more than fresh air, good smells, beautiful sights, and a place to garden. It gives inspiration for art works. The special shape of stone walls on Martha's Vineyard inspired the quilt pictured and spring flowers inspired the banner. Nature imagery appears often in this book: a great blue heron, shells, and fish from Florida, frogs inspired the cover-up, and flowers prompted Leslie Master's banners. Projects give more pleasure if they have an idea behind them in addition to their purpose.

Like the author's Michigan deck, you can treat yours as an outdoor room using indoor and outdoor fabrics.

Project 6:

Stone wall quilt

Sarah Westlake and I traded art works. She gave me a handsome painting in exchange for this quilt designed after the horizontal stone walls near her island summer house. It's not a literal depiction but a stylized one, horizontal bands for rock with small pieces inter-stitched, a band of stormy sky at the top (the sky top is down in the photo), and a band of dried leaf mulch at the base.

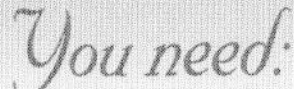

Quilt size 42″ x 67-1/2″, wide rows 7-1/2″ x 42″, narrow rows 2-3/4″ x 42″ (pieced)
Backing. Gray-blue fabric 44 ″ x 69″
Wide rows:
- *Dark gray-blue fabric. 8″ x 44″*
- *Striped gray and white fabric. 17″ x 44″*
- *Speckled gray/white fabric. 17″ x 44″*
- *Dark gray textured fabric. 8-1/2″ x 34″*
- *Brown paisley fabric. 8″ x 44″*

Narrow rows. Assorted-colored fabric 3-1/2″ x 1-1/2″ to 5-1/2″
Quilt batting
Thread
Tools: scissors, hand sewing needle, ruler

LEFT: This quilt features horizontal patched rows in gray, blue, and brown stone shades like the rock fence shown. Loaned by Sarah Lance Westlake.

ABOVE: The square-cut rock walls of Martha's Vineyard provided inspiration for the quilt design. Photo by Merle Westlake.

Your fabric stash

Fabrics come in the wonderful range of quilting cottons and poly-cottons available in stores. Like most stitchers I have stacks, drawers, cupboards full of fabrics saved over the years. I needed both stores and stash for this collection of stone colors and textures. You won't be able to find the exact ones listed for many of the projects in this book, so collect up what you can and compose from there. Colors always depend on each other to be bright or dark, intense or muted. Be sure your colors all relate to each other to create the effect you want. The quilt is hand-sewn—rare for me but a portable project for vacation time.

Sewing the quilt:

1. Assemble the pieces in each row. Lay pairs of pieces face-to-face, seam, open, and press seam allowances to one side. Join pieces until the row is formed.
2. Join the rows: Once the rows are assembled and seams pressed to one side, align and sew the rows together.
3. Add the backing and filler. I prefer quilts without a binding because this makes such a narrow frame. To make this kind of edge, lay batting flat and smooth it out. Lay the quilt faceup on the batting and smooth it. Lay the backing on the quilt face-to-face. Smooth them all flat and trim the quilt bat to fit.
4. Pin the edges across the seam line. On the bottom begin 12″ from the corner, sew toward the corner, and around three sides, stopping 12″ into the bottom edge for the opening to turn. Sew three stitches across corners as you sew. Turn the quilt right-side-out, clip corner seam allowances, smooth it flat, and pin the layers with safety pins. Sew the opening closed.
5. Quilt the layers. Machine or hand stitch across each seam. Sew vertical lines in the wide rows.

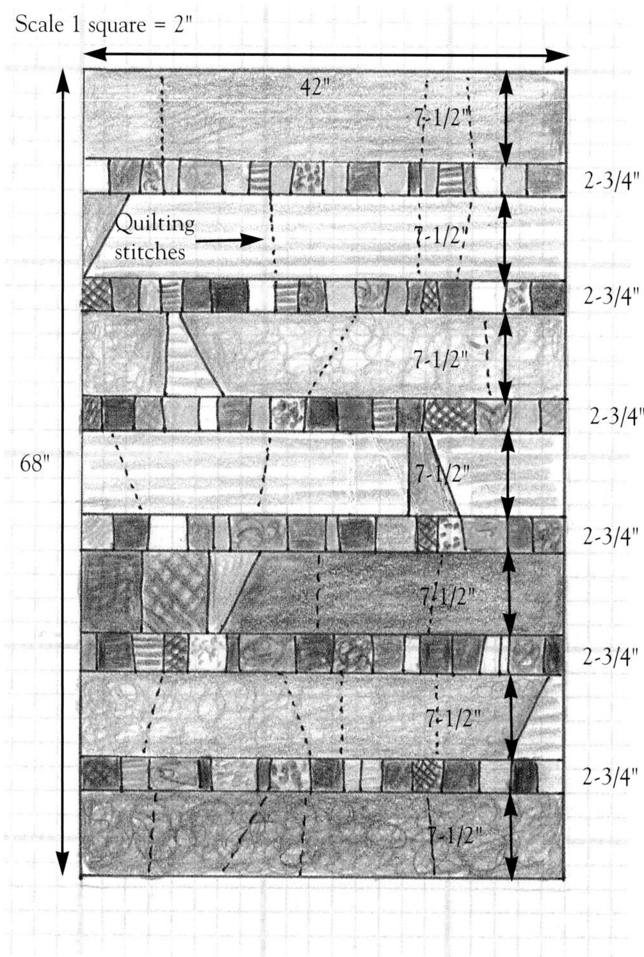

Project 7:

Glider seat & cushions

The glider cushions shown took less than a day to make, but every piece of outdoor furniture has different requirements. This one required a thin cushion so it wouldn't be too high. Some are designed for thicker cushions... or their owners have longer legs than I. Some are designed as slings with sturdy fabric for support such as deck chairs. Some furniture comes with a slot for sliding a new cover in when the old needs replacing. All cushions and outdoor fabrics last longer if they can be brought inside when not in use, or at least seasonally.

Removable cushions of poly-cotton upholstery fabric, foam, and fiberfill, come inside as a rule but can stand a rain shower or two.

About outdoor fabrics

The outdoors is hard on fabrics. To withstand the elements a fabric should not absorb water, resist deterioration and fading in sunlight, and not mildew. Generally this means synthetic materials. In the local fabric store you can find several choices. Woven acrylic is one of the best and comes in canvas-type weaves with good colors and designs. PVC non-woven fabric is plastic molded to look like fabric with openings between fibers for air circulation. Vinyl-coated fabric is much like upholstery leatherette except lighter weight. It is waterproof, non-porous, and doesn't "breathe" (meaning you might stick to the seat).

Padding for your cushion presents another problem. You hope the water will run through and not give you a soggy bottom when it looks deceptively dry. The glider has a polyurethane sponge cushion which will dry if left out. Both urethane and coated fiber are available at fabric/craft stores. Ideally, cover the fiber or foam with a layer of fiberfill.

You can use interior upholstery fabrics outside under a covered porch or take the pieces inside when not in use. The glider fabric shown is a poly-cotton blend of drapery/light upholstery weight chosen for its subtle colors. You can make fabric waterproof with an iron-on vinyl coating by HeatnBond. A silicone spray coating (like Scotch-Guard) will make fabric water and stain repellent but not waterproof.

Heavy and synthetic fabrics may require a leather or heavy-duty needle. Manufacturers continue to develop new fabrics for improved sewing and performance.

Plan seat cushions

How much fabric do you need? Consider these factors: The cover should fit snugly to avoid wrinkles. Every seam requires added seam allowances. Most upholstery fabric is designed to run across the seat and up the back and comes about 57″ to 60″ wide. Welting, an attractive feature consisting of covered cord inserted in the seams, takes extra fabric. Do you want the cover to be removable? How will cushions stay on the chair or glider?

This simple cushion has no welting and minimal seams with ties or loops to hold it on. Like most covers, it has a zipper-type closing to insert the foam. Use existing cushions for a pattern or measure the seat width and depth. Test a padding on the seat for thickness and try the chair (as did Mother Bear). Too high? Too hard? Too bulky to store? Cut the foam padding 1/2″ to 1″ larger. An electric knife is good for this. If you plan to wrap with fiberfill, cut the foam to size and add the layer of fiberfill.

To estimate fabric amounts, measure each pattern piece needed and draw a diagram to place them for cutting on-grain. Add more for design repeats if needed.

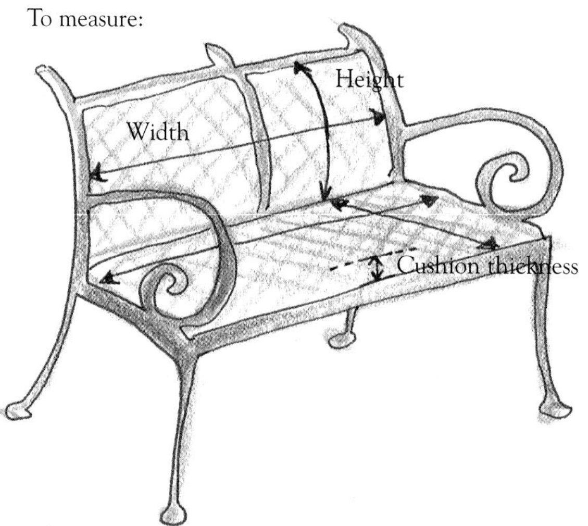

PATTERN:

Measure for your own pattern:

Seat width. Add the seat width, plus the cushion thickness, plus two 1/2″ seam allowances (i.e., seat width 37″ + 1″+ 1/2″ + 1/2″ = 39″).

Seat depth: For a no-seam wrap cushion add the seat depth twice, plus twice the cushion thickness, plus seam allowances of 1/2″ (i.e., 17-1/2″ + 17-1/2″ +1″ + 1″ + 1/2″ + 1/2″ = 38″). Measure back cushions in the same manner. Add 1″ for a zipper placket.

Cut the seat (with the grain or pattern) 39″ x 39″, cut eight ties 9″ x 2-1/4″, cut two back covers 20″ x 38″, cut two 2″ x 4″ tabs.

You need:

Fabric (for the glider seat and back, plus a pillow). 2-1/3 yards x 50″
Zipper. 36″
2 zippers (optional). 18″
Thread

Foam padding to size. One seat 18″ x 39″, two backs 18″ x 19″
Vinyl-coated fabric (or other fabric). 19″ square
Stuffing for pillow
Tools: sharp scissors, tape measure, metal yard stick, pencil, zipper foot, electric knife

Sewing the covers:

1 Measure foam padding to fit slightly larger than finished cushions. Cut foam straight up and down with scissors or electric knife or have the fabric store cut the foam to size.

2 Make the ties: Fold a 3/4″ double hem to cover raw edges. Topstitch.

3 Seat cushions: Lay the Tabs face-to-face with the zipper ends and sew across close to the zipper. Unfold.

A. Align the zipper edge with the seat back edge face-to-face, including tab.

B. Open flat and topstitch the fabric edge. (For a zipper placket, don't open, but fold the seat fabric to cover the zipper. Press and topstitch fabric 1/2″ from the folded edge.)

C. Align the zipper with the other seat edge face-to-face. Pin, sew, open flat, and topstitch.

D. Open the zipper. Align the seat side seams and sew a 1/2″ seam allowance.

E. To make a boxed corner, fold the front corner to match seams. Draw and sew a diagonal line. Clip off the extra. Repeat. For the back corner, fold the corner side seam to zipper seam, draw the diagonal line, and clip off about 1/4″ to make a slot for the ties. Fold a tie to make a loop, insert the tie ends, ties inside, and sew. Repeat. Turn right-side-out.

F. Insert the foam padding and zip closed.

4 Back cushions: Same as above. For the ties, measure the size loop or tie needed and insert them as described. The loop is a folded tie. Insert the foam padding and hand sew the seam closed.

Pillow: Two 20″ squares of contrasting fabrics, 18″ square pillow stuffing, and thread.

To make the pillow on the back, draw a line from corner to corner both ways for four triangles. Match opposite color squares face-to-face and sew across diagonally, 1/2″ on each side of the line. Cut between the stitch lines, unfold, and press open. Match seamed squares face-to-face, opposite colors aligned. Sew seams across 1/2″ from each side of the seam line. Cut along the seam line, open, and press.

Align the seamed squares face-to-face and sew the edges. Begin 3″ from one corner, sew four rounded corners (1/2″), and stop sewing on the fourth side, 3″ from the corner for an opening to turn. Insert the pillow stuffing, fold a hem, and sew closed with hidden stitching.

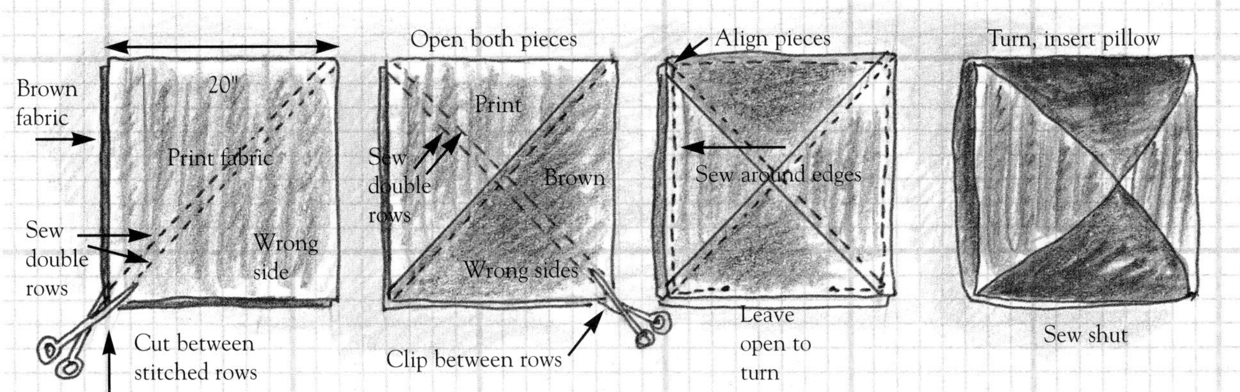

Project 8:

Garden banner

Flags and banners, from team logos to seasonal imagery, birthday messages, and more, decorate homes, lawns, and even cars. For a special personalized one, design your own. Wording on double-sided translucent flags will appear in reverse on the opposite side, so you may choose to stick with pictorial imagery. Double-sided cut-away appliqué is not for beginners! To make flags more easily, paint on the imagery or appliqué pieces to both sides of the banner and satin-stitch the outlines.

RIGHT: Stiff nylon flag fabric makes an enduring outdoor banner. Double-sided appliqué is difficult but worth it for your personal banner.

BELOW: Use tear-away backing with appliqué to stabilize the satin-stitching.

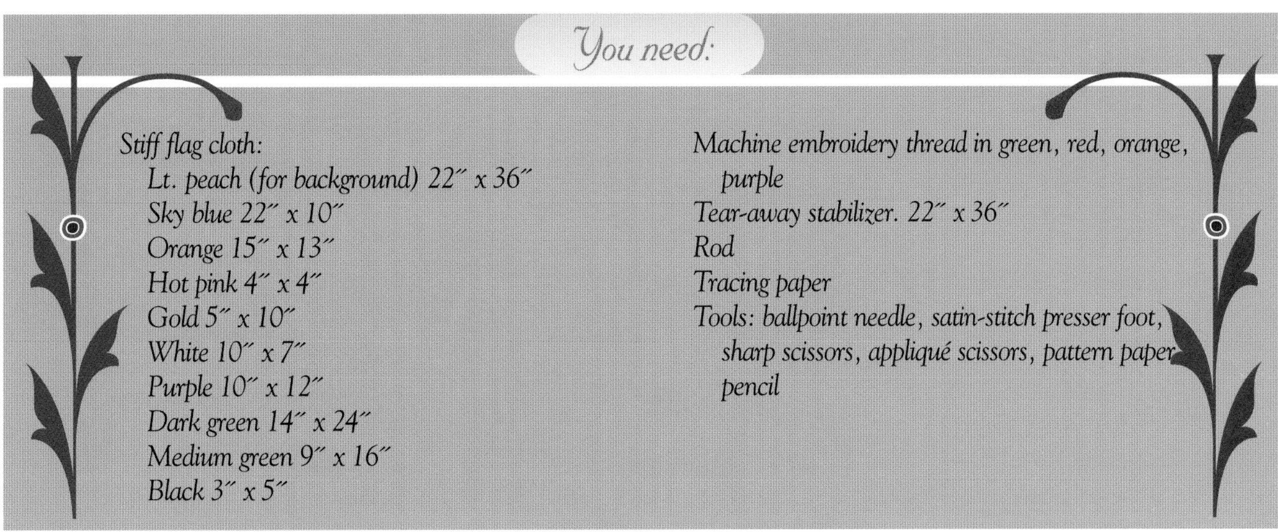

You need:

Stiff flag cloth:
- *Lt. peach (for background) 22″ x 36″*
- *Sky blue 22″ x 10″*
- *Orange 15″ x 13″*
- *Hot pink 4″ x 4″*
- *Gold 5″ x 10″*
- *White 10″ x 7″*
- *Purple 10″ x 12″*
- *Dark green 14″ x 24″*
- *Medium green 9″ x 16″*
- *Black 3″ x 5″*

Machine embroidery thread in green, red, orange, purple
Tear-away stabilizer. 22″ x 36″
Rod
Tracing paper
Tools: ballpoint needle, satin-stitch presser foot, sharp scissors, appliqué scissors, pattern paper pencil

MAKING THE PATTERN: Enlarge the diagram given to size on paper by photocopy or grid. For your own design use simple shapes wherever possible. Small or long, narrow ones may fray and are difficult to sew.

Trace the pattern pieces onto the fabric. Where pieces overlap add a 1/4″ seam allowance to both colors. Cut out the pieces.

Sewing the banner:

1 Background: Align and join the sky blue fabric to the peach background. Fold and sew a narrow hem up both sides. Fold a double 2″ hem in the top edge to align over seam line 1/8″ and topstitch.

2 Appliquéing the pieces:

A. Lay the background over the pattern. Place pattern pieces on the background, overlapping them 1/4″, and pin. To keep them in place lay tracing paper over all, pin, and free-motion machine baste them. Remove pins and tear off the paper.

B. Pin the banner to the tear-away stabilizer to keep satin-stitching from puckering the fabric, which it will certainly try to do.

C. Put the same color thread in both the bobbin and machine to satin-stitch around each object. Choose a brighter shade of the same color to satin-stitch. Make a double row to cover if needed.

D. Turn the banner, tear away backing, and trim away the background behind each color. Use the appliqué scissors designed to do this, or sharp scissors. Use extreme care to cut away only the extra fabric. (I cut through the face fabric twice. Notice those wide outlines in places? Cover-ups.)

E. Slide the rod in the slot.

A sharp sewing machine needle alleviates fabric snags and pulls. Appliqué scissors work best for trimming away layers of fabric.

Flag fabrics:

Two special fabric types are available for making flags. Flag fabric, or sport cloth, is a stiff nylon, translucent in light for a stained glass window effect. It resists fading and sews fairly easily. It remains stiff and smooth in all weather. The other more common fabric, usually polyester and used for lining as well, is softer in hand and thus harder to sew. It can be used for windsocks and even banners.

Both of these fabrics need hemming. Sport cloth frays and polyester needs stiffening. Seams should be serged, French seamed, or flat fell seamed due to weather wear and visibility from both sides.

Double-sided banners made by appliqué with the underneath fabric cut away require great care and time in construction. Only the stiff nylon works. To hold the narrow overlapped seams, a wide satin-stitching is needed. This outlining always puckers without stabilizer backing.

Scale 1 square = 1"
Rod slot double
20"
38"
Orange
Dark green
Purple
Medium green
Orange
Hot pink
Purple
Orange
Medium green
Dark green
White
Medium green
Hot pink
Purple
Purple
Purple
Dark green
Hot pink
Medium green
White
Orange
Thread
colors
indicated
Orange

Project 9:

Flower basket

We are enjoying an era of elegant fabrics reminiscent of the 1880s that produced crazy quilts full of rich, wonderful textures. Now we can weather-proof some of these wonderful materials to use outside. This begins with manufacturing where fabrics and ribbons are made of synthetics rather than silk. Wires woven or sewn into ribbon edges keep them from drooping. The mattelesse fabric, normally soft, stands stiff and perky with clear vinyl coating ironed on before finishing the edges. Use a ready-made wire frame basket and weave in a seasonal collection of ribbons. To make leaves or petals, iron vinyl coating (HeatnBond) onto the fabric, cut out the shapes (a long football), and finish the edges (or not). Pinch a double fold in the leaf to shape it, then wire several leaves and petals into a bouquet.

Weave ribbons around a wire basket and decorate it with a fabric flower stiffened with iron-on vinyl.

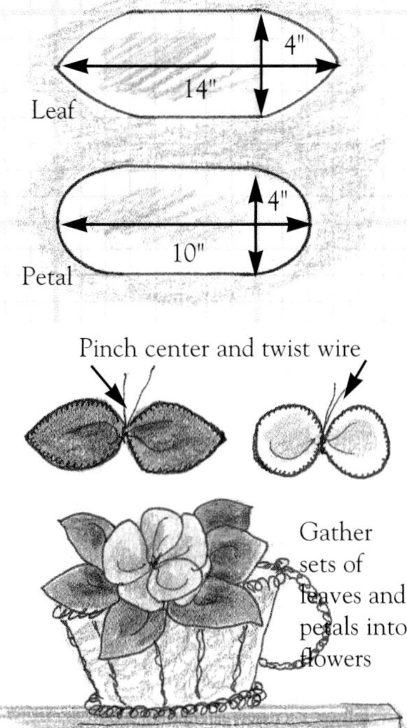

Chapter 4

Sewing for a Barbecue

Photographed at Rand and Pat Hall's Barbecue

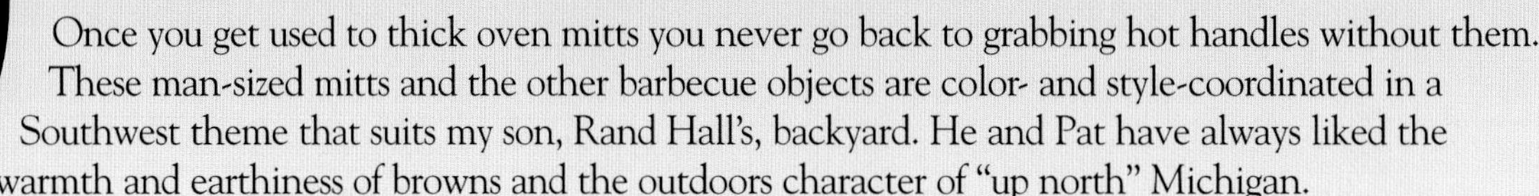

Once you get used to thick oven mitts you never go back to grabbing hot handles without them. These man-sized mitts and the other barbecue objects are color- and style-coordinated in a Southwest theme that suits my son, Rand Hall's, backyard. He and Pat have always liked the warmth and earthiness of browns and the outdoors character of "up north" Michigan.

A few yards of canvas in Southwestern colors give Rand and Pat Hall's barbecue a coordinated outdoor look.

Project 10:

Barbecue mitts

Anybody can buy ordinary oven mitts, so I aimed for some new ideas. I discovered Thermal Fleece, a lightweight metallic-coated insulating material that deflects cold. Alas, this polyester product melts in heat—not good for mitts—so three layers of quilting fleece were used. Hey, let's do Western-style fringes! I found a supple polyester imitation leather that would be easy to sew. But on second thought, fringes could prove both messy and flammable, so that idea died, too. As a result, these mitts of desert-hued cotton canvas have simple Western-style cuffs.

You need:

Each mitt:
Printed cotton canvas 12″ x 18″
Plain canvas (for lining) 12″ x 18″
Three layers cotton or polyester fleece (for filler) 18″ x 36″ (one package HTC Craft and Quilting Needle-punched Fleece)
Leather or leatherette (for cuffs and tab) 14″ x 16″
Leather sewing machine needle
Strong thread
Brown or maroon thread
Tools: sharp scissors, pattern paper, pencil, pins

PATTERN: Enlarge the pattern (see page 34 for the mitt pattern), or make a pattern with a 1″ border around your hand. Cut out two mitts and two linings, one in reverse. Cut out two cuffs 7″ x 7″. Filler pattern, add 3″ of cuff to the mitt and cut three layers. Hanging tab cut 2″ x 4″ leather.

Rand Hall dons a canvas apron and quilted mitts. He is ready to barbecue his specialty—salmon steaks.

Making the mitt:

1. Align the cuff and mitt top edges face-to-face and sew. Align the cuff and lining and sew.
2. Lay filler on the lining to half way up the cuff, fold the cuff over it, and pin the layers together. Repeat.
3. Topstitch a quilting design to bond the layers on the mitt and cuff.
4. Tab: Double-fold the tab lengthwise and topstitch.
5. Align the mitts face-to-face. Fold and pin the tab in the mitt seam on the thumb side. Sew around the edges of the mitt. You won't be able to serge the inside of the thumb because the corner is too sharp. Sew this thumb seam double with short stitches to hold securely. Trim seam allowances, thumb corner seams especially.
6. Turn right-side-out. Hah! This is easier said than done. Begin by poking the end of the thumb inward. Then use a stick to push through. At the top push your hand into the glove to start. Reach inside and pull it right-side-out. Put your hand inside to push all the seams smooth, especially the thumb.

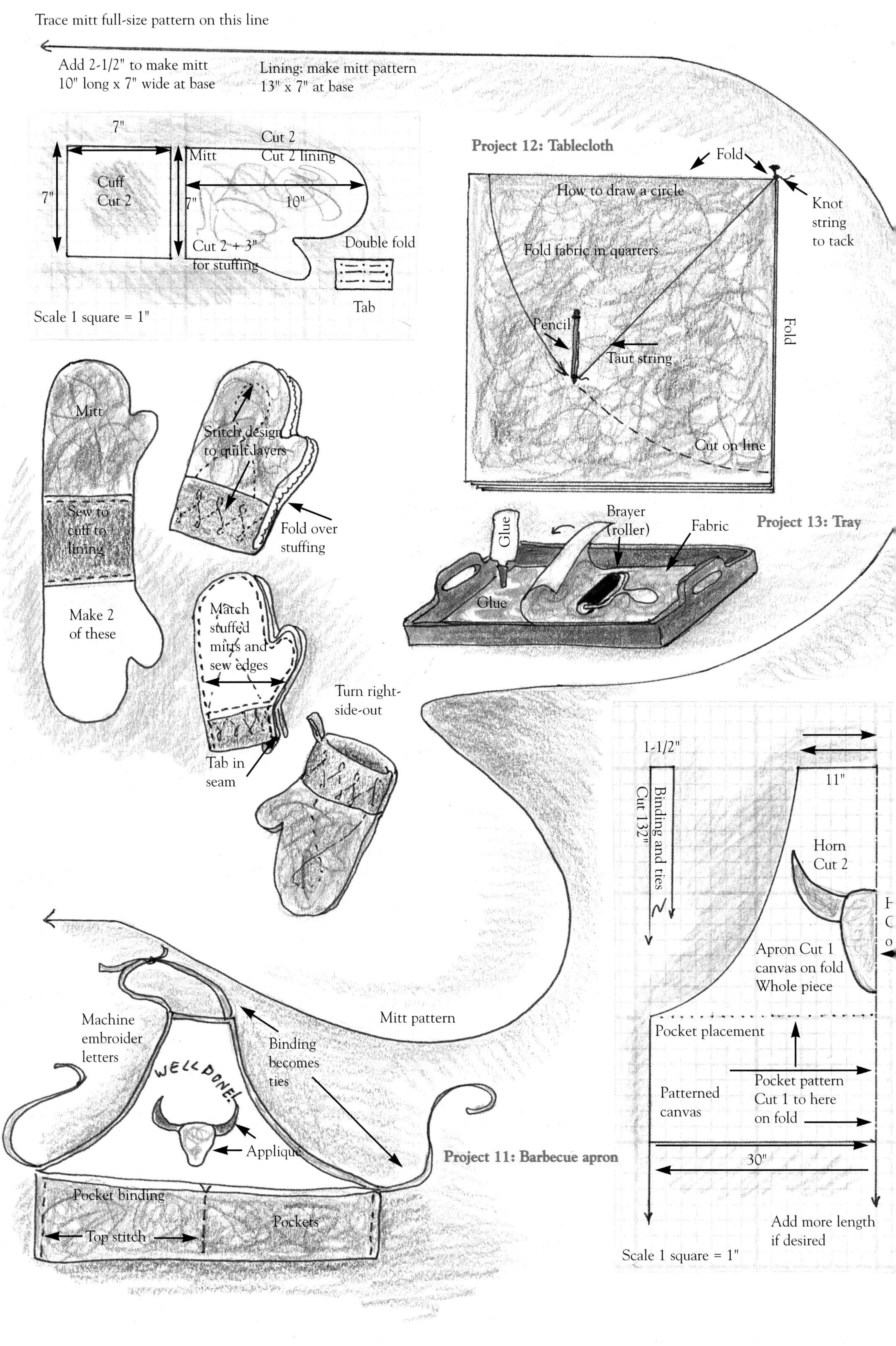

Trace mitt full-size pattern on this line

Add 2-1/2" to make mitt 10" long x 7" wide at base

Lining: make mitt pattern 13" x 7" at base

7"

7"

Cuff
Cut 2

Mitt

Cut 2
Cut 2 lining

7"

10"

Cut 2 + 3" for stuffing

Double fold

Tab

Scale 1 square = 1"

Mitt

Sew to cuff to lining

Make 2 of these

Stitch design to quilt layers

Fold over stuffing

Match stuffed mitts and sew edges

Tab in seam

Turn right-side-out

Project 12: Tablecloth

Fold

How to draw a circle

Knot string to tack

Fold fabric in quarters

Pencil

Taut string

Fold

Cut on line

Glue

Brayer (roller)

Fabric

Project 13: Tray

Glue

1-1/2"

Binding and ties
Cut 132"

11"

Horn
Cut 2

Apron Cut 1 canvas on fold
Whole piece

Pocket placement

Patterned canvas

Pocket pattern
Cut 1 to here on fold

30"

Add more length if desired

Scale 1 square = 1"

Machine embroider letters

Binding becomes ties

Mitt pattern

WELL DONE!

Appliqué

Project 11: Barbecue apron

Pocket binding

Top stitch

Pockets

Project 11:

Barbecue apron

Grease spatters and mustard stains, but looking "cool" is important. So here's a man's barbecue apron with an ambivalent message... which you can change to one of your own. The waist is a low-slung male fashion on this pattern. A sketch shows how to alter this. This is a quick, easy pattern. The same fabrics used for the mitts are used here.

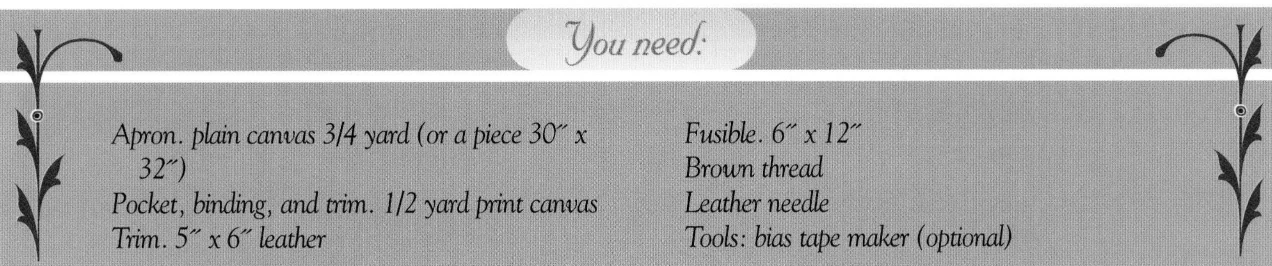

You need:

Apron. plain canvas 3/4 yard (or a piece 30″ x 32″)
Pocket, binding, and trim. 1/2 yard print canvas
Trim. 5″ x 6″ leather
Fusible. 6″ x 12″
Brown thread
Leather needle
Tools: bias tape maker (optional)

PATTERN: Enlarge the pattern given, or measure from the drawing (see page 34 for the apron pattern). Apron 30″ wide x 24″ x 11″ across the top. Finished pocket 8″ x 24″. Alter at will; make the waist higher, the apron longer, the top shorter. Pocket cut 8-1/2″ x 30″ printed canvas. Add no seam allowances (unless you plan to hem edges).

Straps and binding: Three strips printed canvas 1-1/4″ x 44″, one strip white canvas 2″ x 30″. (If you are not using a bias tape maker you may wish to cut these strips 2″ wide for easier handling.) These strips are not cut on the bias as most binding because the curve is gentle enough not to need this flexibility.

TRIM: Steer head (enlarge the pattern) 5″ x 6″ (cut one) printed canvas, horns 2″ x 5″ (cut two) leather

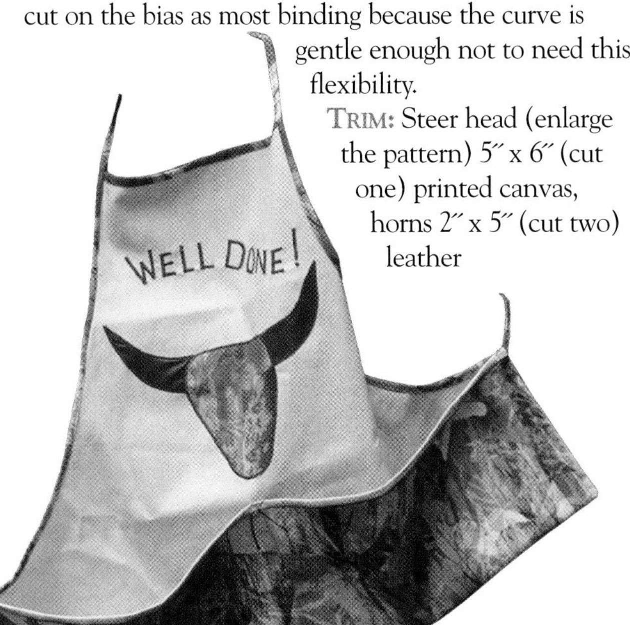

Sewing the apron:

(See page 34 for a diagram.)

1. Appliqué the steer head pieces in place, using fusible to bond. The thick fabrics don't require stabilizer backing to prevent puckering. Draw your message in straight lines because circles are harder to sew. Satin-stitch the edges and sew the letters.
2. Bind the apron across the top edge. Match the binding face-to-face with the apron and sew a 1/4″ seam allowance. Fold a 1/4″ hem in the binding, fold it over the seam allowance, and topstitch on the binding or in the ditch for a more finished look. At the apron left side, fold the binding over and sew to the top (about 21″). Continue sewing the binding to make the neck strap. Sew the right strap to 21″, pin the binding to the apron, and sew. The binding up the sides becomes neck straps.
3. Bind the pocket top with the plain canvas binding. Fold and sew the apron waist ties and clip this strip in half.
4. Pin each waist tie to the apron binding end at the sides. Align the pocket face to **back** with the apron bottom edge and pin, including the tie. Serge or sew the sides and bottom edge. Turn the pocket right-side-out.
5. Finishing: Topstitch the pocket sides and up the center to form two pockets. Note that the pocket center stitching pattern provides reinforcement. Try on. You're cool!

Project 12: Tablecloth

Several patterns for tablecloths appear in this book because they have great utility as well as the ability to transform an ordinary table into a style statement. Furthermore, they provide a sanitary cover for a picnic table. Making this tablecloth is easy.

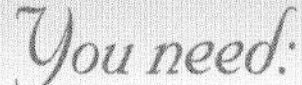

You need:

For a full 60″ circle, take 60″ of 60″ wide fabric. If you must add pieces on the sides you will need nearly twice as much fabric. To buy exact amounts, make a diagram on graph paper with a compass and measure.

FABRICS: The fabric shown is a heavy-weight printed canvas treated to repel stains. The goal is to go as long as possible without having to wash it—just dab off stains with a sponge. Selection was based on pattern and color to harmonize with the scene... and isn't that how we make so many fabric selections?

PATTERN:

1 Measure the table:

A. Round tables: Measure across the tabletop for the diameter. Measure down from the table edge how much "drop" you want. Tablecloths on page 67 go all the way to the floor, but these decorative tablecloths can get in diners' way. A drop too long may catch on clothing and pull off the table. A drop too short looks skimpy. Usually 8″ to 15″ looks good as well as covers the table and diners' legs. Try fabric on your table to decide. Add the diameter and twice the drop for the cloth size. To make a circular pattern, tape a thumbtack (point up) on the floor. Fold your fabric in quarters, reverse side out, and lay the fold point at the pin point. Over the tack point, put the hole in your yardstick or a knotted string and measure out to the length (half the diameter plus drop). Hold a pencil on the mark and draw a circle, or pull the string taut, looped around the pencil, and draw the circle. (See page 34 for a diagram.)

B. Oblong tables: An oblong, a stretched-out circle with rounded ends, is measured like a circle. The width constitutes the diameter of the circular ends. For the width, measure the diameter and drop as above. For the length, add twice the drop to the length measurement. Cut the cloth to the length and round the circular ends as above.

C. Square and rectangular tables are easy: Measure across and add twice the drop. Evenly split added fabric.

Making the tablecloth:

1 Cut the circular pattern from your fabric. Add side pieces if the fabric is not wide enough. Pieces are added to each side to keep the seam lines even on the tabletop. To piece, pin paper to the incomplete circle, draw the completed circle line, and use this pattern to cut the added pieces. Be sure to add seam allowances.

2 By far, the easiest way to hem a circular cloth is serging set to 3 thread short stitching. If the fabric is thin do a rolled hem. If not use a flat hem. With a sewing machine you can do a rolled hem, sew on bias tape, or add decorative trim or fringe.

Project 13: Tray

This project is an easy one—no sewing, just gluing and varnishing. You can refurbish an old tray or color-coordinate a new one with your decor. Hey, even your barbecue setting can have a decor instead of a pick-up look!

You need:

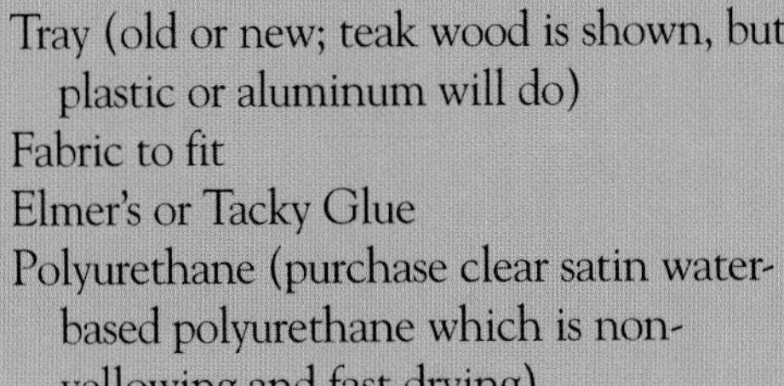

Tray (old or new; teak wood is shown, but plastic or aluminum will do)
Fabric to fit
Elmer's or Tacky Glue
Polyurethane (purchase clear satin water-based polyurethane which is non-yellowing and fast drying)

Tools: nylon paint brush, utility knife or single-edge
razor blade, rotary cutter or scissors, roller, sponge and water, scraper

To make the tray:

(See page 34 for a diagram.)

1. Wash the tray and, if you are using wood, sand it as needed for a smooth, clean surface to work on.
2. Cut the fabric to fit with a straight sharp edge. Dampen the fabric.
3. Cover the tray with glue. Work fast, or sprinkle a little water on if needed. Use the scraper to spread glue evenly.
4. Position the fabric right-side-up on the glued tray. From the center, use hands and roller to smooth fabric to the edges and push out all air bubbles. The glue will come through the fabric. Mop it up with the sponge. The glue will darken the fabric colors slightly.
5. When the glue is nearly dry, roll out and flatten any air bubbles in the surface. Push the fabric toward the edges with your fingertips to stretch the fabric. Use a new razor blade or utility knife (with new blade) to cut along the fabric edge to trim off any extra. The blade must be sharp or you'll pull out threads and mar the smooth cut. Peel out the extra fabric.
6. Once the tray has dried, paint it with several coats of clear polyurethane. Read the can for instructions such as air temperature, stirring, thickness of coats, etc. Work outside for ventilation, but don't leave the piece in direct sunlight.

Chapter 5

Sewing for the Beach

Photographs of Hattie and Brad at Siesta Beach

Beach-time ranks high as an all-time favorite. There's water, sand, shore grass, birds, shells, sea sounds, breezes, everything to entertain. Some things make this scene even better: a hat to keep the sun off, a cover-up to dry off after a swim, a towel to lie on, and a tote to carry all of this stuff to the beach.

Hattie and Brad Stroud are outfitted for winter break on Siesta Key Beach with a sun hat, tote, towel, and frog cover-up.

Project 14:

Floppy beach hat

You need:

Fabric in denim, canvas, cotton, or poly-cotton. 24″ of 44″
Interfacing for stiffness or lining for quilting. 16″ x16″
Thread to match
Tools: scissors, paper

Recognize that zippy '60s-style fabric used for this wide-brimmed floppy sun hat? Maybe your fabric stash has a similar treasure.

FABRICS: This hat fabric, from my stash, is a brash 1960s print of brilliant colors and bold design resembling designs by Mary Mecko, a Scandinavian designer.

PATTERN: Make a paper pattern. Adjust it to fit your head. Add 3/8″ seam allowances for serging or seaming.
Cut two brims and one interface, one crown and one top.

Sewing the hat:

1 Join brim seams to make a circle. Repeat. Align brims face-to-face, seams matched, add interfacing, and seam the outside edge. Trim seam allowances, turn, and press. Try it on. Trim the edge if it's too small. Widen brim seams if it's too large.
2 Sew the crown seam to fit the brim opening.
3 Align the top in the crown face-to-face. Pin, stitch, turn, and press.
4 Topstitch the brim edge or pin the layers to stabilize and quilt.
5 Align the brim to the crown, pin, and sew. Topstitch the seam allowance to the crown or sew on a grosgrain ribbon hat band.

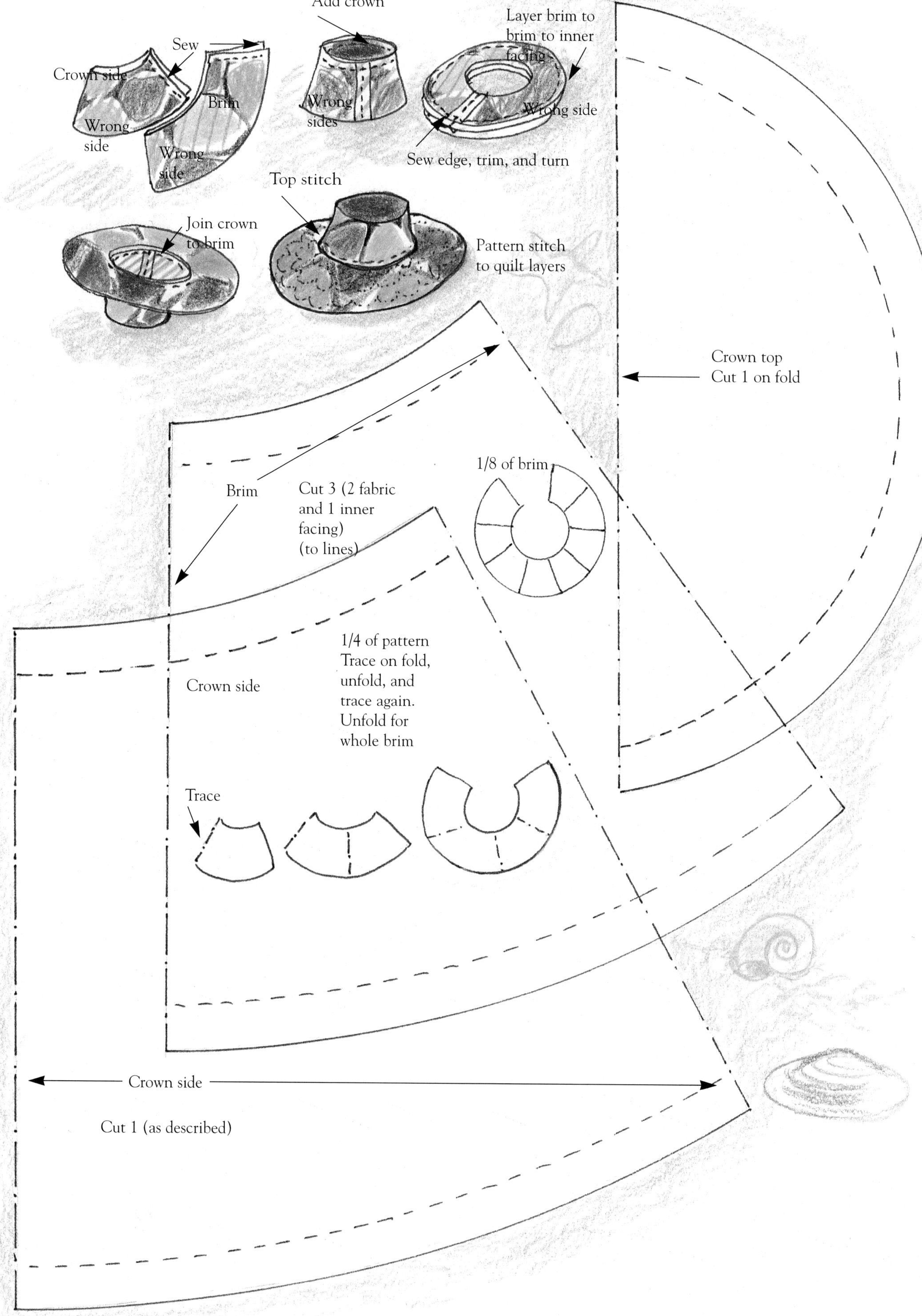
Add crown
Layer brim to brim to inner facing
Sew
Crown side
Brim
Wrong side
Wrong side
Wrong sides
Wrong side
Sew edge, trim, and turn
Top stitch
Join crown to brim
Pattern stitch to quilt layers
Crown top
Cut 1 on fold
1/8 of brim
Brim
Cut 3 (2 fabric and 1 inner facing) (to lines)
1/4 of pattern
Trace on fold, unfold, and trace again.
Unfold for whole brim
Crown side
Trace
Crown side
Cut 1 (as described)

Project 15:

Beach tote

Here's that '60s fabric again. I never throw anything out! The waterproof lining, an Italian-made raincoat fabric, has vinyl laminated to a lightweight knit. Don't iron it and do use tracing paper on it when stitching, or buy HeatnBond vinyl, a clear thermo-web to laminate your own fabric on either side.

Vinyl-coated fabric lining keeps wet towels or suits from dripping through this tote. Add interfacing or quilt stuffing for a less floppy bag.

You need:

Canvas-weight fabric. 36″x 44″
Waterproof fabric (for lining). 26″x 44″
Velcro. 1″ x 1″
Thread
Tools: yardstick, sketch paper, pencil, quilt pins, tracing paper

PATTERN: Draw directly on the fabric back. (For a directional print add 1/2″ seam allowances at the bag bottom and cut each bag side design upward.) Do not pin through waterproof fabric. Cut one bag, one lining, one pocket, and two handles. (Use interface for a stiffer bag.)

Sewing the bag:

NOTE: To be waterproof, the lining is sewn separately and joined to the bag.

❶ Triple-fold the handle, raw edges first, for six thicknesses 1″ wide and 36″ long. Topstitch both edges and pattern-stitch the center. Cut in half. On the bag face, loop the handle down from the top 6-1/2″ from each corner, ends over the top 1″, and sew to join on the seam line.

❷ Match lining sides face-to-face. Pin only in seam allowances. Sew the side seams. Align the bag corner seams and stitch. Turn bag right-side-out.

❸ Fold a double 1-1/2″ hem on the pocket top and scallop-stitch the hem. (Line the pocket with vinyl if you wish.) Lay the pocket on the bag face-to-face with the pocket bottom edge 15-1/2″ down from the bag top edge. Topstitch and fold the pocket up onto the bag and pin the side edges. Sew Velcro patch on the pocket center top and the matching bag side.

❹ Align bag sides face-to-face. Pin and sew the side seams. Align and sew one corner seam, leaving the other open to turn.

A. Match the bag and lining top edges. Put the lining in the bag face-to-face, tuck in the handles with 1″ ends sticking up, and align the side seams. Pin in the seam allowances and sew the top edges in 1/2″.

B. The tricky part: Reach into the open bag corner seam and pull the lining through to turn the bag right-side-out. Tuck the lining into the bag and fold the top edge flat. Topstitch around the top 1/2″ from the edge.

C. To shape the bag, fold the bag side seams. Include the lining for 2″ at the top, then pull it out of the fold. Topstitch in 1/8″ from top to the corner, pivot, and refold to stitch, and pivot and refold to sew up the side. Tuck in the corner seam allowances on the other side and repeat.

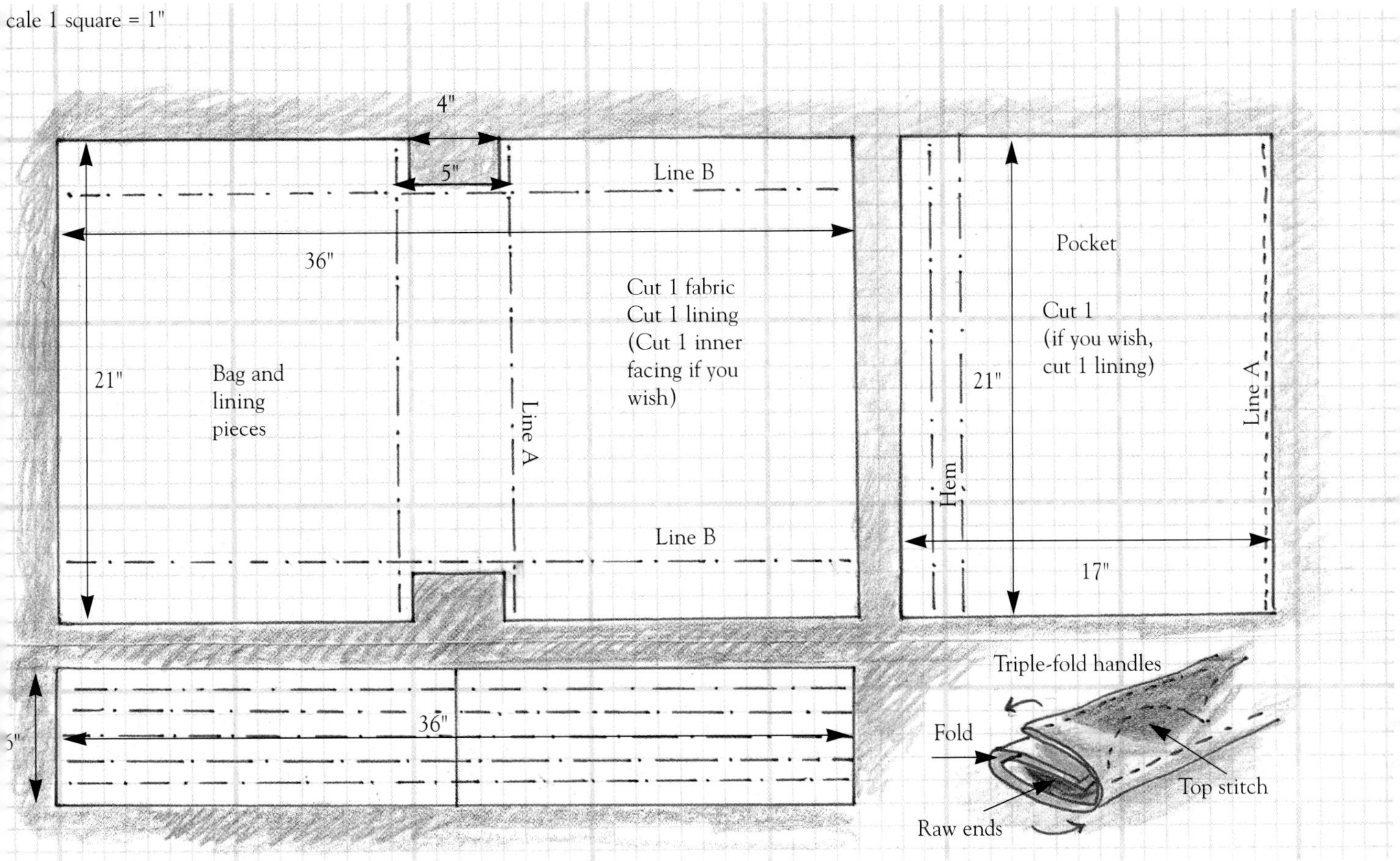

cale 1 square = 1"

4"
5"
Line B
36"
Cut 1 fabric
Cut 1 lining
(Cut 1 inner
facing if you
wish)
21"
Bag and
lining
pieces
Line A
Line B

Pocket
Cut 1
(if you wish,
cut 1 lining)
21"
Line A
Hem
17"

6"
36"

Triple-fold handles
Fold
Top stitch
Raw ends

Project 16:

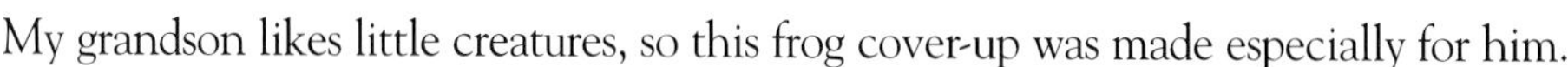

Frog cover-up

My grandson likes little creatures, so this frog cover-up was made especially for him.

Hattie models Brad's frog cover-up with her hands snug in the frog's.

Wrap up in a terry cloth beach cover-up and pretend you are a frog!

You need:

Green terry cloth. 50″ x 44″
1 yellow hand towel
Black felt. 2″ x 4″
Dark green felt. 11″ x 18″
HeatnBond fusible. 2″ x 4″
Thread to match
Golden-yellow machine embroidery thread
2 black buttons (1/2″)
Dab of fiberfill
Tools: sturdy scissors or rotary cutter, paper for pattern, pencil, pins

Beach fabrics

This knitted cotton terry with a loop face is less apt to snag than a woven terry but is heavier weight to work with. The yellow is a cotton towel terry and the dark green is cotton/rayon felt. The frog could be made in stretch velour, Polarfleece, or another soft, fluffy fabric. Terry is best for absorbing water.

Note: With heavy fabric you need to grade the seams (trim away extra) where several thicknesses are sewn.

MAKING THE PATTERN: For the frog, measure a 44″ square with rounded corners, or measure your child from head top to outstretched finger tips and add a few inches. Frog (cut one), visor 6″ x 14″ (one green and one yellow), eyes 3-1/2″ x 7″ (two green and two interfacing), eyeball (two 2″ circle black), hands 7-1/2″ x 9″ (two yellow and two dark green).

For the hands, trace the pattern for two yellow terry hands. Cut two green 9″ x 11″, but do not cut out the hands yet.

Sewing the frog:

1 Eyes: Use iron-on adhesive or machine baste the black eyeball on the eye. Satin-stitch to outline and appliqué with golden yellow embroidery thread. Sew an arrow-shaped highlight. Repeat for the other eye. Back the eye with interfacing and fold double, eyeball inside. Sew around the edges, leaving the base open to turn. Trim seam allowances narrow to minimize bulk and turn. Repeat.

2 Visor: Match the green and yellow visor pieces face-to-face, sew the front edge, and turn. Pin so the yellow lining is exposed 1/2″ on the green side and topstitch on the seam. Topstitch the yellow fabric raw edge in 1/2″.

3 Nose: Embroider two nostrils or sew on buttons.

4 Head/Visor:

A. On the visor, pin the eyes, lightly stuffed, face-to-face and centered 4″ apart, raw edges aligned. Match the visor and frog face-to-face (including eyes) and pin. Serge or sew across the visor top. Continue this serging around the frog. Or fold a 1/4″ hem and zigzag all around the edge.

Note: My serger balked at this many-layered seam. You will need to grade seam allowances to sew the seam.

B. Turn the visor right-side-out and topstitch across the top, in 1/2″ to cover lining raw edges.

5 Hands:

A. Fold and stitch a 3/4″ hem at the yellow hands' wrists. (The green aren't cut out yet.) Pin the yellow hands on the cover-up visor side, 1/2″ from each corner edge, and machine baste. Satin-stitch the raw edges with gold-colored thread.

B. Pin the green hands on back, covering the yellow hands' seams, and pin in the center. Use green thread on top and bobbin to sew around the yellow hands. Turn over and use sharp or appliqué scissors to trim away felt outside the stitch line.

Threads

Threads exist for every fabric need: cotton-coated polyester for strong general sewing, lustrous machine embroidery threads for satin-stitching, tough polyester threads for long wear, slender mono-filament threads for hidden stitching, metallic threads for decoration, woolly nylon loosely spun threads for serging a rolled hem, waxed threads for hand quilting, double-weight buttonhole thread... and more. Sewing machines also have needles to match, from fine to sturdy diameter sharps, ballpoints, large holed to metallic thread holed, leather blade, and double needle, among others. It helps to choose the right thread and right needles for the project.

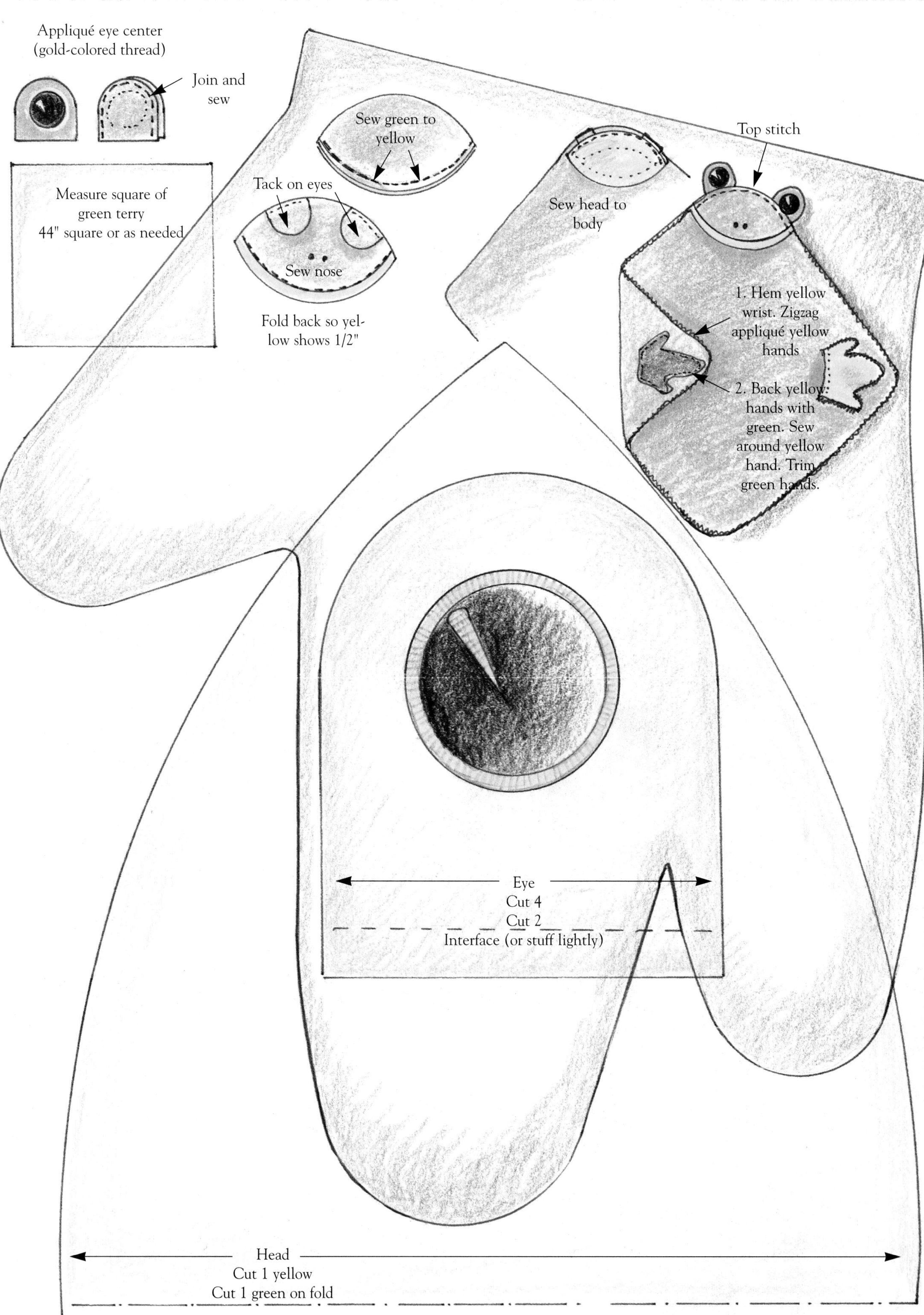
Appliqué eye center (gold-colored thread)
Join and sew
Measure square of green terry 44" square or as needed
Sew green to yellow
Tack on eyes
Sew nose
Fold back so yel- low shows 1/2"
Sew head to body
Top stitch
1. Hem yellow wrist. Zigzag appliqué yellow hands
2. Back yellow hands with green. Sew around yellow hand. Trim green hands.
Eye
Cut 4
Cut 2
Interface (or stuff lightly)
Head
Cut 1 yellow
Cut 1 green on fold

Project 17:

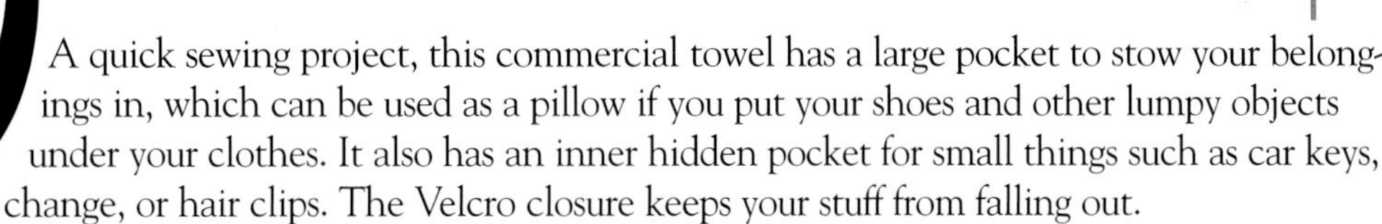

Beach towel

A quick sewing project, this commercial towel has a large pocket to stow your belongings in, which can be used as a pillow if you put your shoes and other lumpy objects under your clothes. It also has an inner hidden pocket for small things such as car keys, change, or hair clips. The Velcro closure keeps your stuff from falling out.

Hattie stows her clothes in the beach towel's Velcro-closure pocket so she can use the mound it makes for a pillow.

You need:

1 large bath or beach towel. 28″ x 53″
Pockets
Hot pink fabric 17″ x 23″
Blue fabric 10″ x 13″
Green fabric 10″ x 13″
Yellow fabric 5-1/2″ x 8″ (hidden pocket)
Velcro strip (or plastic zipper or snaps). 1″ x 16″
Tools: scissors, ruler, pins

Scale: 1 square = 1"

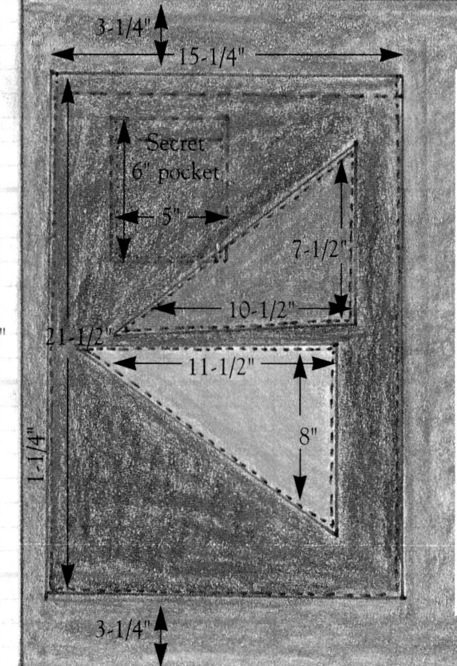

FABRICS: Some towels have face and reverse sides, such as velour. There is no right side to the sport polyester fabric, but right sides are indicated in case another fabric is used.

PLAN YOUR DESIGN: Shown is an abstract sailboat, but you can create your own design: large initials, a fish, a swimmer, a palm tree, a flower, a car or motorcycle—the list goes on. Simplify the design to something easy to hem (straight edges), or use iron-on fuser and appliqué the design in place with satin-stitching.

PATTERN: Inside pocket 6″ x 8″ yellow, large pocket 17″ x 23″ hot pink, sail triangle 9″ x 12″ green and 7″ x 11″ blue

Sewing the towel:

1. Fold a 1/2″ hem all around the hidden pocket and press. Double-fold the open end, hem, press, and sew. Place the hidden pocket on the towel, 4″ down from the top and 5″ in from the right side. Topstitch in 1/8″, leaving the hem open. Add Velcro, a zipper, or snaps, if you wish.
2. Large pocket:

A. Measure pocket placement 1-1/4″ from the top and 3-1/4″ from each edge. Sew the Velcro strip on the towel, 1-1/4″ from top edge and 3″ from the right side.

B. Motif: For the sails, cut a triangle measuring 9-1/2″ x 12″ (green) and 7″ x 11″ (blue). Fold and press a 1/4″ wide hem on all sides. Pin the sails on the large pocket and topstitch. The only tricky part is folding the sharp corners to hide the hem. Fold over the tip of the sail to the hem line, then fold the hems, and trim seam allowances at an angle. Tuck in the ends with a long pin as you sew.

C. Large pocket: Align the upper Velcro strip to the right end of the large pocket face-to-face, overlapping 1/2″. Sew along the Velcro edge 1/8″. Fold the Velcro back onto the pocket and topstitch 1/8″ in on the Velcro to make a 1″ wide hem. Fold and press a 1/2″ hem around the remaining three sides of the pocket.

D. Stick the pocket Velcro strip to the towel strip and pin the pocket in place. Topstitch in 1/8″.

Project 18:

Sandbags

This is a good project to teach young stitchers to use the machine. Few toys lasted more years and got more use with my kids and grandkids than these simple sandbags. To make sharing easy, choose assorted colors and patterns. Children can imagine them to be bunkers, walls, building stones, tiny beds or furniture, bean bags to toss, or loads for toy trucks to carry.

Kids can help sew and fill sandbags with sand or pellets for creative toys that last for years.

You need:

Fabric. 6″ x 42″ (6″ x 7″ for each bag; sewn bags measure about 3″ x 5-1/2″)
Thread
Sand or plastic Poly Pellets
Clean, dry play sand is best. (We've used wet, dirty sand when impatient. The bags do dry but they are still dirty!) Find plastic pellets at crafts stores. Also possible are lentils, navy beans, alphabet pasta, even sugar or salt, but you can imagine the problems with moisture or mice.
Tools: rotary cutter or scissors, funnel

FABRIC: Choose tightly-woven poly-cotton so the filler doesn't sift out.

Make the bags:

1. Tear the fabric, or use a rotary cutter or scissors to make squares.
2. Fold the bag face-to-face, matching 6″ edges. At the fold, sew in 1/4″ to the corner, pivot, and stitch to the top. No need to clip threads, just chain bags together to sew them all.
3. Kids like this part. Clip bags apart and turn each right-side-out. Use a funnel to fill the bags half full of sand or pellets. Tuck the raw ends in 1/2″, fold flat, pin, and sew the top shut.

Chapter 6

Sewing for Your Patio

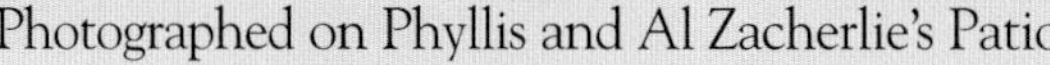

Photographed on Phyllis and Al Zacherlie's Patio

Sheer voile and lace fabrics impart a romantic quality to Phyllis and Al Zacherlie's patio setting on Sarasota Bay.

Project 19:

Cover-up

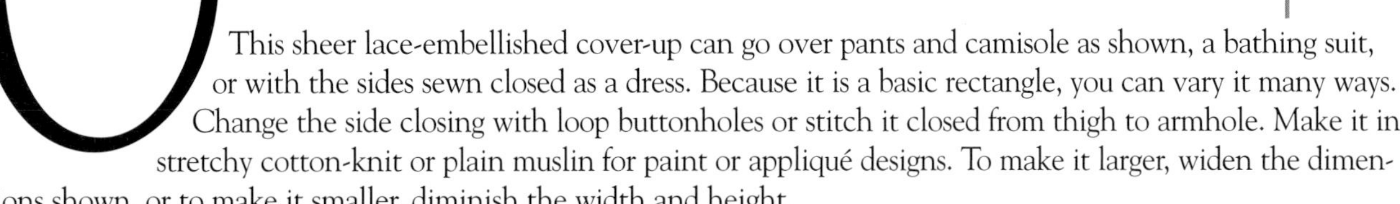

This sheer lace-embellished cover-up can go over pants and camisole as shown, a bathing suit, or with the sides sewn closed as a dress. Because it is a basic rectangle, you can vary it many ways. Change the side closing with loop buttonholes or stitch it closed from thigh to armhole. Make it in stretchy cotton-knit or plain muslin for paint or appliqué designs. To make it larger, widen the dimensions shown, or to make it smaller, diminish the width and height.

FABRICS: There's something so romantic about sheer fabrics. The cover-up, tablecloth, napkins, and hat were all made from the same four poly-cotton voile fabrics. In sewing, this softly-woven fabric can shift and its seams pucker. Keep the fabric taut while sewing seams, with hands fore and aft of the machine needle. Read your machine manual for advice on handling lightweight fabrics—the results are worth it. The iridescent lace comes as yardage with one finished edge. Some lace-woven net is designed to be cut into strips.

PATTERN: Measure diagram dimensions directly on the fabric, adding 1/2″ to 5/8″ seam allowances. French seams and flat fell require the full 5/8″.

Pattern pieces: A- white top section, B- fold-over collar cut on the bias, C- green triangle in the center, D- iridescent lace overlay, E- pink lower section, F- lace overlay strip, G, H, I and J are border bands, and K- ties (1-3/4″ x 36″). Cut two of each (in reverse) for the back, except the collar. Cut out all pieces.

Phyllis' sheer voile cover-up, a simple rectangle, could be made in a variety of fabrics from stretchy spandex to painted silk or muslin.

Seams

Sheer fabrics expose the seam allowances. Various kinds of seams can hide, finish, or strengthen these seams.

Serger: *It is easiest to align pieces face-to-face and serge. This machine cuts off an even seam allowance and overcasts it all in one step. Seam allowances can be left as is or ironed flat and topstitched in place. Adjust the differential feed to avoid puckering or stretching seams. Serge sheer edges with a rolled hem or a flat three-thread hem.*

Sewing Machine Flat Fell: *Align pieces face-to-face to straight stitch. Fold a hem in the seam allowance to tuck the edges in and topstitch.*

French Seam: *Align pieces back-to-back. Machine sew 1/4˝ outside the marked seam line. Trim the seam allowance to 1/8˝ and fold the fabric face-to-face. Press the seam and sew 1/4˝ from the edge. This works best with straight seams.*

Hidden Seam: *Align the collar (or border) face-to-face and sew one edge to the cover-up. Trim this seam allowance to 1/4˝ and press it toward the collar. Press a 1/4˝ hem in the collar's other edge and align this hem overlapping the seam line 1/8˝. Topstitch in the ditch or hand sew with hidden stitches.*

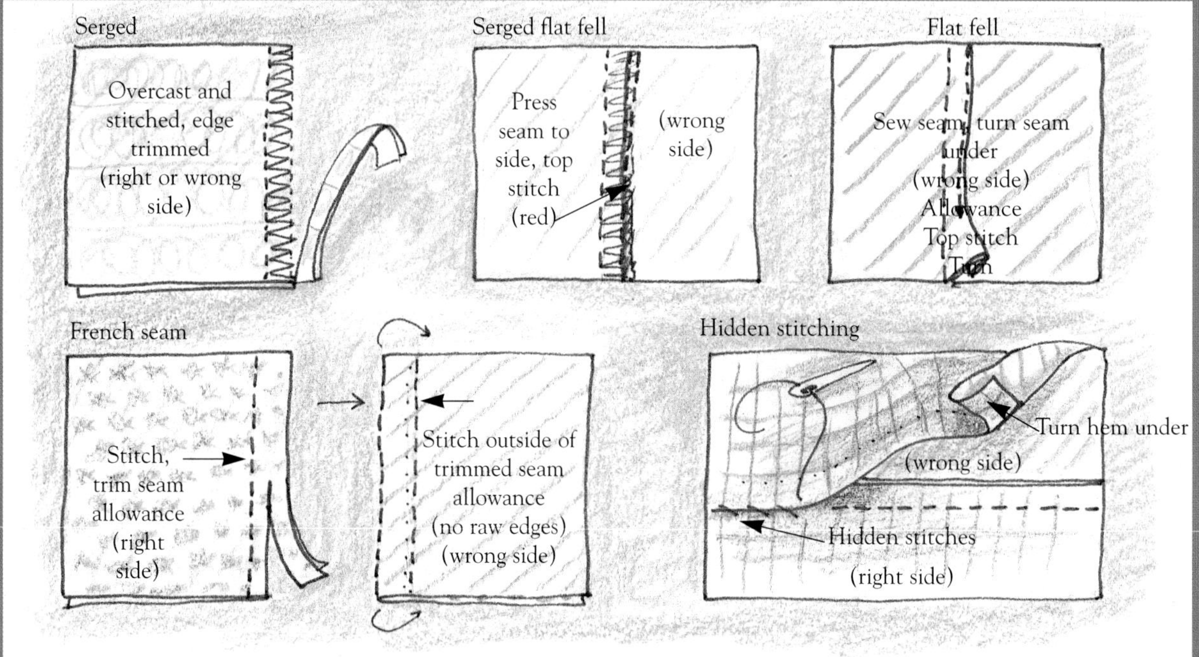

You need:

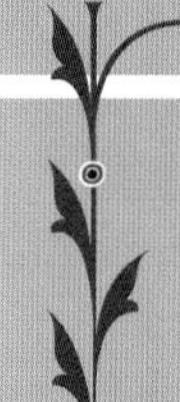

White print poly-cotton voile. 22˝ x 30˝
Pink poly-cotton voile. 46˝ x 44˝
Green poly-cotton voile. 66˝ x 30˝
Lace. 7˝ x 72˝ (or 14˝ x 36˝)
Iridescent lace. 22˝ square
Off-white sewing thread
Tools: scissors, 24˝ x 60˝ paper for pattern, yardstick, pencil

Making the cover-up:

1 Overlays: Sew lace to C and E.

A. Press and lay the front flat and squared. Lay lace F strips on the pink, top edges aligned, and pin or baste. Pin and topstitch the lace lower edge to the voile. Keep fabric taut, but don't pull against the feed dogs, just help guide the fabric through.

B. Lay the green front flat and squared, add the lace triangle, side edges meeting, and pin or baste. Fold a 1/2˝ hem and topstitch.

2 Color sections: Join pink E to green C and green C to white A, both front and back. These are bias seams so do not stretch them in sewing. Repeat for back.

3 Align front and back pieces and sew the shoulder seams. Cut the neck hole to fit you. Leave it wrong-side-out.

4 Sew across the ends of the collar B to make a circle. Press and turn right-side-out. Fold the collar lengthwise and tuck it into the neck hole, centering the collar seam on the back. Serge or sew to join. Turn the cover-up right-side-out, fold collar seam allowances down, and topstitch in place. **Note:** For a hidden joining

seam here (and on the borders), unfold the doubled collar, align the lower edge to the cover-up face-to-face, and serge or sew. Iron a hem in the raw collar edge. Pin the hem, overlapping the joining seam, and topstitch in the ditch to hold the seam in place.

5 Borders:

A. Seam the border strips to make long strips as needed, H to I and J to J, to make one long strip. Press. Fold right-side-out lengthwise and press.

B. Align the border H-I edges to the cover-up face-to-face with the H-I joining seam at the tip of the green C triangle and serge or sew. Trim the seam allowance, fold back, and topstitch.

C. Match the border G to the cover-up, mark the length, and seam both ends. Turn and press. Sew the border G to the cover-up face-to-face by serging or as noted in Step 4.

6 Ties. Measure a 40″ string for 36″ tie. Fold the tie K over the string lengthwise, secure at one end, and sew a 3/8″ pocket the full length. Pull the string to turn the tie. If the string comes loose use a knitting needle to turn. Tie a knot in one tie end and clip off evenly. Fold tie, align on the border at the hip (triangle tip), and topstitch in place.

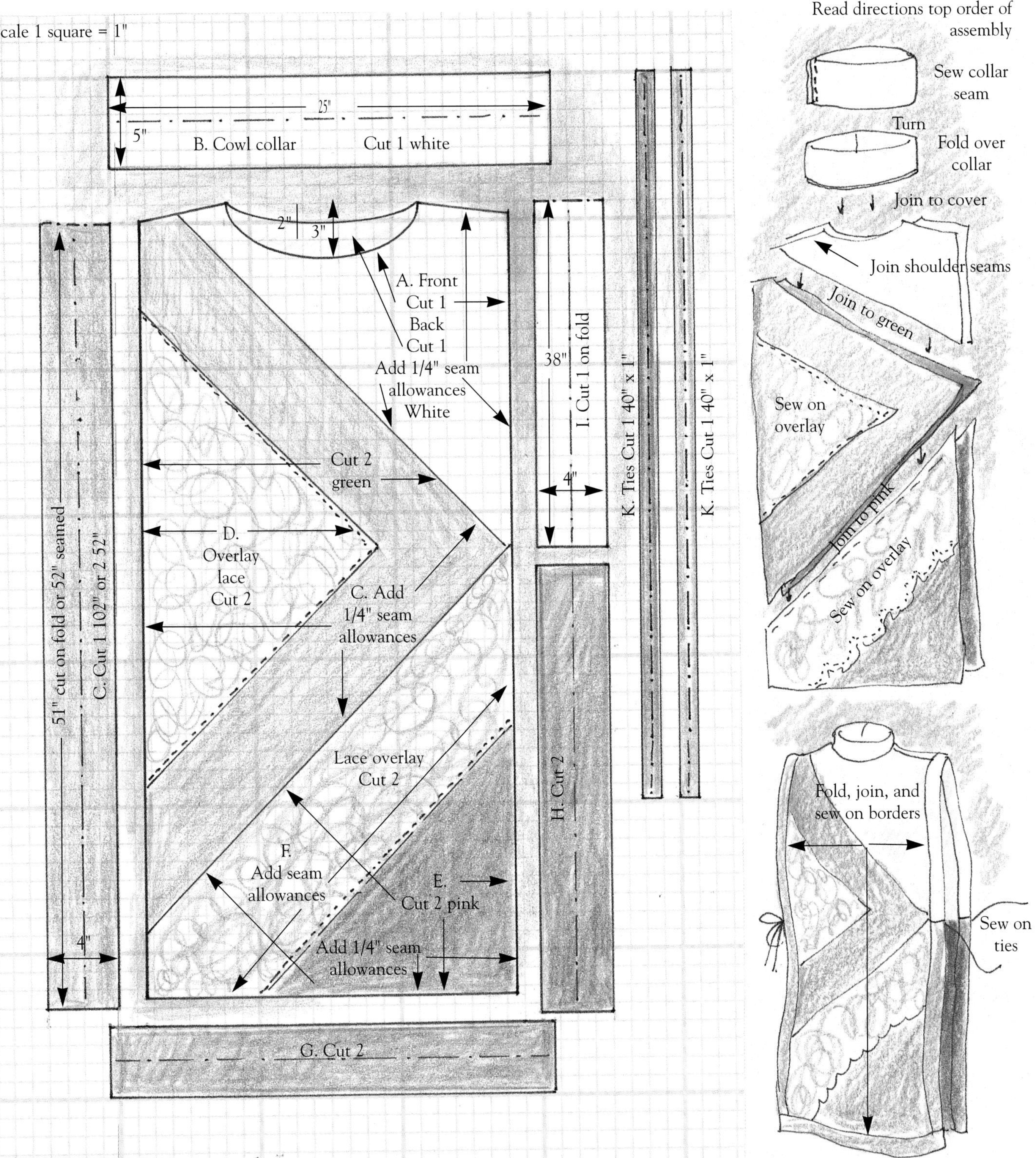

Project 20:

Tablecloth

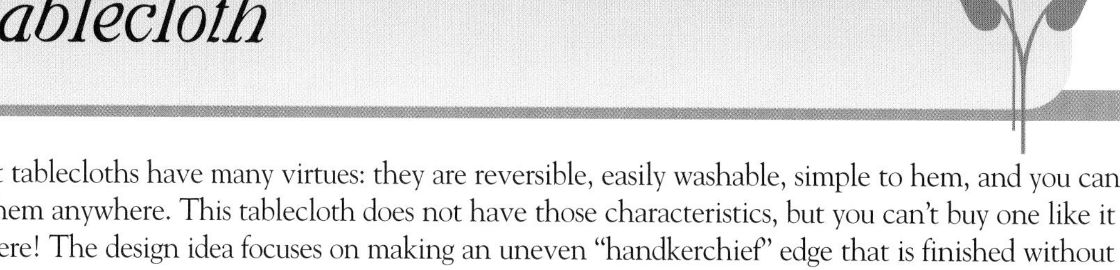

Most tablecloths have many virtues: they are reversible, easily washable, simple to hem, and you can buy them anywhere. This tablecloth does not have those characteristics, but you can't buy one like it anywhere! The design idea focuses on making an uneven "handkerchief" edge that is finished without a final hem. I like puzzles, and making this tablecloth is somewhat like solving one—the pieces have to go together in the right order in order to sew straight-across seams.

Like putting puzzles together? Make this patchwork voile and lace tablecloth in eight sections.

You need:

Yellow poly-cotton voile. 4 yards x 45˝
Green poly-cotton voile. 1/2 yard
Tissue-weight metallic fabric. 16˝ x 24˝
2˝ wide lace. 2-1/2 yards

Light yellow thread
Tools: sharp scissors, metal yardstick, pencil, paper for the pattern, tear-away backing paper

FABRICS: For strength in the sheer voile seams all pieces are doubled. This intensifies the colors in some pieces as well as supports the metallic fabric which could fray. You could use a single layer of heavier-weight fabric or eight square handkerchiefs in silk, embroidered, or bandanna-style.

NOTE: This is not a reversible tablecloth because the raw seams appear on the back. Serge the seams or trim and overcast them.

PATTERN: A 1/8 section is given with dimensions for the pattern pieces you need. Draw this full size and use it for a guide to cut pattern pieces and in constructing sections. Make sure the angles of your pattern are correct. Align pieces with the grain as marked. Cut eight pieces of these: lace B, lace C, gold D, gold E, yellow lining D, yellow lining E. Doubled pieces: Cut eight green on the fold, eight A yellow on the fold.

Sewing the tablecloth:

NOTE: Assemble pieces in the order given so you have straight seams to sew.

❶ Make 1/8 sections:

A. Yellow F squares: Fold to make a square, hem one side from fold. Trim the edges, turn right-side-out, and press.

B. Green points: Use tear-away backing paper. Fold the green A piece, iron, and stay stitch the raw edges outside the seam line. On all eight sections lay the green A fold on the right so the on-grain edge stabilizes the bias edge when joined later.

C. Lace overlays: Lay lace B in place on A. If this seam puckers, use backing paper. Topstitch lace B in place. Lay lace C on green A, overlapping the end of B. Topstitch.

D. Match gold D to its lining and pin. Align the top edge of D (and its lining) with the bottom edge of A/C face-to-face. Serge this seam.

E. Match gold E to its lining and pin. Align the left side edge of E (and its lining) with the top right edge of yellow F face-to-face and sew.

F. Align the bottom straight edge of D/C/A/B with the top straight edge of A/E, matching it at the center seams, and serge.

G. You have now completed 1/8 of the tablecloth. Repeat steps A to F for each of the eight star sections.

❷ Assemble the sections: Align the sections in pairs. Match on-grain edge of the green A with a bias edge of the next A and pin. Match the center seams where gold joins lace and pin. Make sure the gold D and E meet before the end of this seam for a neater joining at the tablecloth edge. Serge or sew the seam. Clip seam allowances at the top (center) of green A. Clip the seam allowances at the yellow end and bartack (zigzag in place).

❸ To complete, join two pairs together in the same manner and clip the seam allowances at the top end of the green. Join the two assembled halves, pin as above, and stitch. (To remove the backing paper, run the closed scissors' tip to score the seam line and pull it away.) Clip the yellow edge seam allowances at a long angle and bartack.

Scale 1 square = 1/2" Diagram for 1/8 of tablecloth Make 8 and join

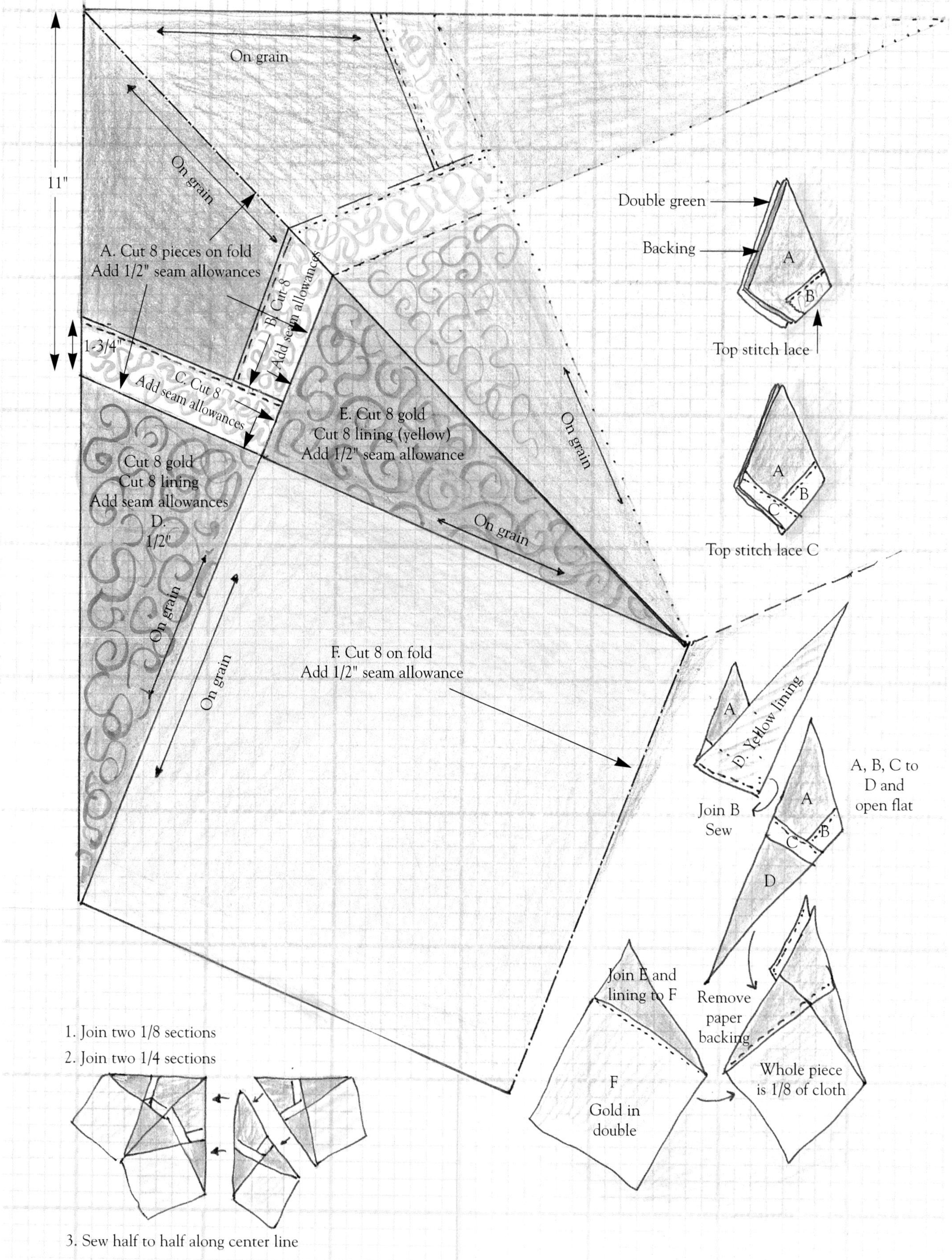

Project 21: Napkins

Matching voile and lace napkins are sewn double diagonally across, cut apart, and unfolded for an easy-to-make project.

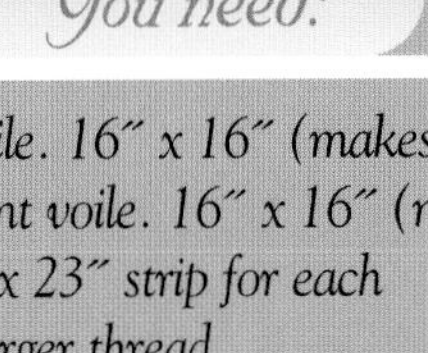

Green voile. 16″ x 16″ (makes two)
White print voile. 16″ x 16″ (makes two)
Lace. 2″ x 23″ strip for each
Woolly serger thread
Tools: scissors, pins

PATTERN: Cut 16″ voile squares and fold diagonally to cut along the fold for triangles. Cut 2″ x 23″ lace strip for each napkin.

TO MAKE: Match a green and a white triangle back-to-back. Lay the lace face-to-face on the white, matching the lace raw edge with the bias edge. Serge or sew, trim 1/4″ seam allowance, and unfold the lace over onto the green. This conceals the center seam. Open the napkin flat and press. Topstitch the lace finished edge to the green. Finish the edges with a rolled hem.

Scale 1 square = 1"   Stack 2 colors   Makes 2 napkins

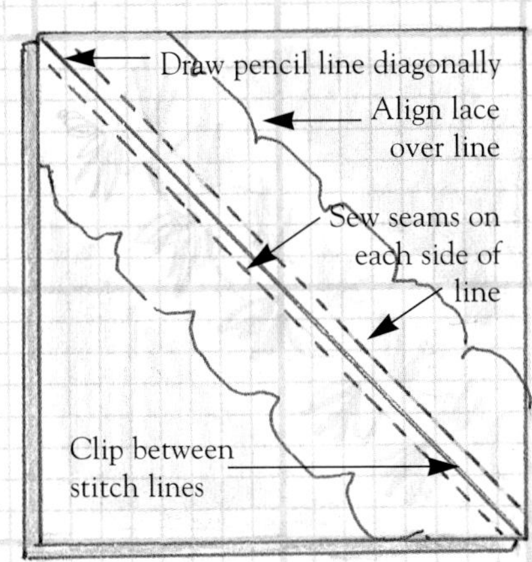

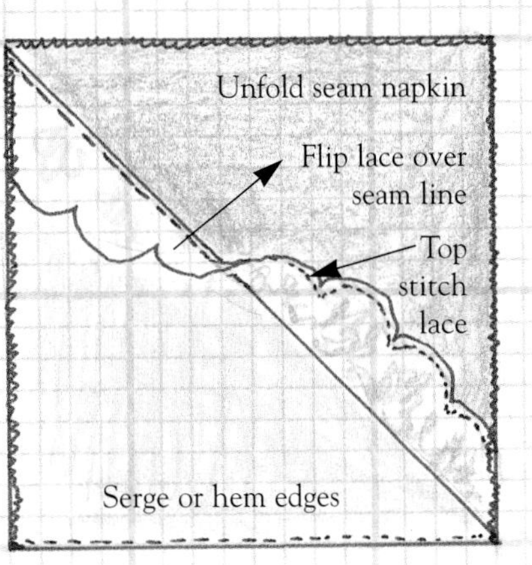

Project 22:

Sun hat

Hats are back in style. They keep off the sun and rain, frame your face, and add color and decoration. This one packs flat but poufs up on the head and tilts at any jaunty angle by bending its wire rim. The voile and lace fabrics give a filtered shade to the face.

FABRICS: This sun hat is made from sheer fabrics, poly-cotton voile, and lace yardage, because of their lightweight and luminescent quality.

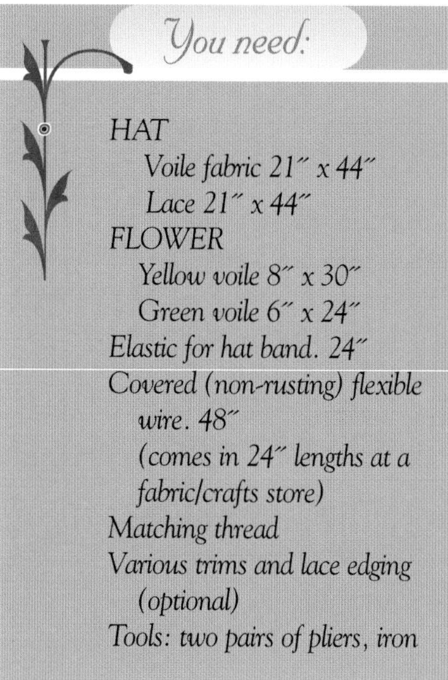

You need:

HAT
- *Voile fabric 21″ x 44″*
- *Lace 21″ x 44″*

FLOWER
- *Yellow voile 8″ x 30″*
- *Green voile 6″ x 24″*

Elastic for hat band. 24″

Covered (non-rusting) flexible wire. 48″ (comes in 24″ lengths at a fabric/crafts store)

Matching thread

Various trims and lace edging (optional)

Tools: two pairs of pliers, iron

Phyllis can shape this sun hat to suit with its fits-all elastic band and flexible wire rim.

MAKING THE PATTERN: Make a paper pattern for crown A, 16″ in diameter, 1/2″ seam allowance included. For brim B, draw a rectangle 4-1/2″ x 44″, seam allowance included. Cut one flower C and eight leaves D (makes four). Cut two crowns A, one of voile and one of lace. Cut two brims B one of voile and one of lace, including its finished edge.

Sewing the hat:

CROWN: Align the two circles back-to-back. Serge the edge or machine baste just outside the stitch line to stabilize.

BRIM:

1. Align the voile and lace lengthwise with the decorative lace edge overlapping the voile edge. If the lace has no decorative edge, add lace edging by topstitching it to the lace edge and continue as above.
2. Topstitch the lace to the voile to make a 1/2″ voile seam allowance inside and a 1/2″ lace edging outside the brim seam.

❸ Fold the brim in half crosswise, match ends face-to-face, and stitch across to make a loop of the brim.

WIRE: Join two wires, overlapping the ends 2-1/2″. Clamp at the joint with pliers or a vice to hold securely. Use the other pliers to twist the ends together until they form a secure bond. Loop the wire overlapping the ends 2-1/2″ and repeat the twist for a 43″ circle. Wrap uncovered wire with a 1″ wide strip of pink voile fabric.

BRIM: Fold the voile and the lace brim back-to-back over the wire circle, aligning the raw edges, pin, and topstitch the lace to the voile 1/2″ from the seamed edge. The lace edge will project 1/2″ beyond this. Serge, overcast, or baste the inner edge of the brim. Align the inner edge of the brim with the edge of the crown, lace-side-to-lace-side, pin at intervals, and stitch.

HAT BAND: Zigzag elastic method: Measure your head size with the elastic and shorten this 2″ or more for a tight fit. Machine sew the elastic ends together. Fold the elastic in quarters and pin. Fold and mark quarter sections on the hat. Align the sections and pin the elastic to the crown/brim seam on the voile side.
Sew on or over the elastic with a wide, long zigzag stitch. Pull the elastic so one quarter of it stretches to meet one quarter of the hat seam. Stretch and sew this way all around the brim.

FLOWER: Cut the Flower pattern from an 8″ x 30″ strip of yellow voile. Fold and align raw edges. Beginning at the fold, sew, basting stitches along the raw edge. Pull to gather the threads as tightly as possible. Twist the fabric in a spiral. Flatten the ends and serge or sew across. Cut four leaves (eight pieces) seam, turn, fold as shown, and stitch across the raw ends. Arrange the flower and leaves, stitch across the ends to hold, and pin to the hat.

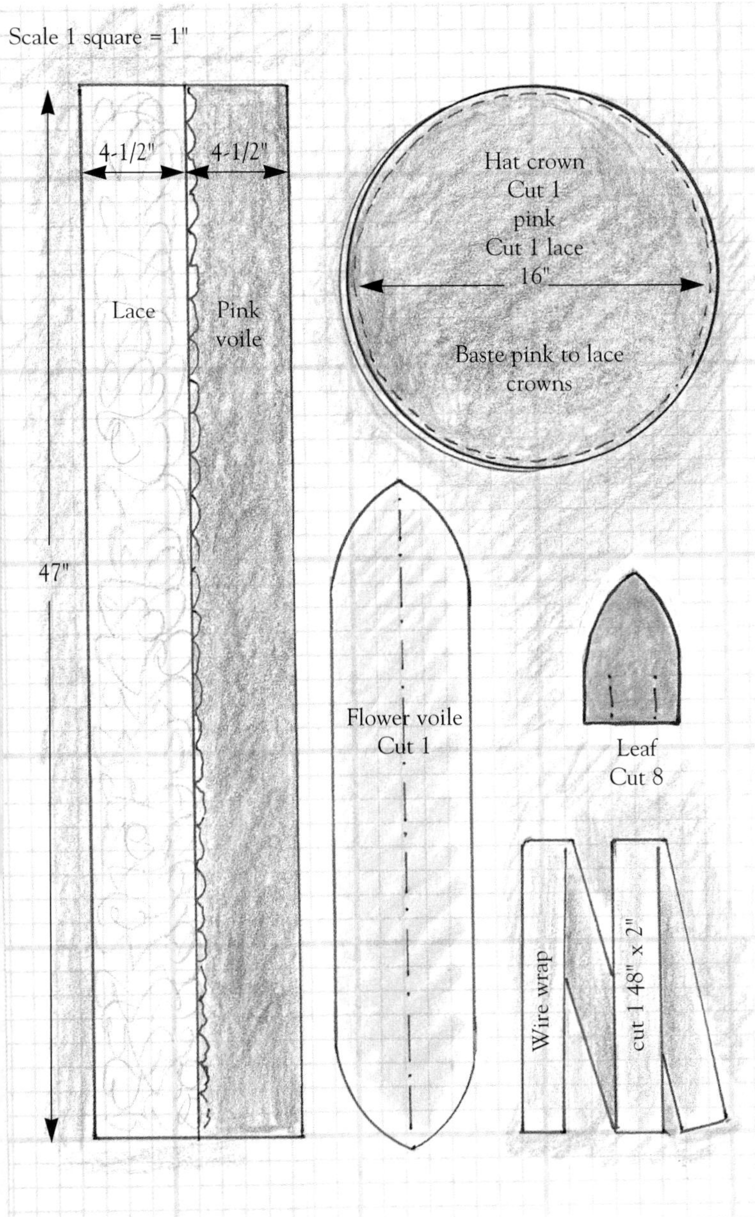

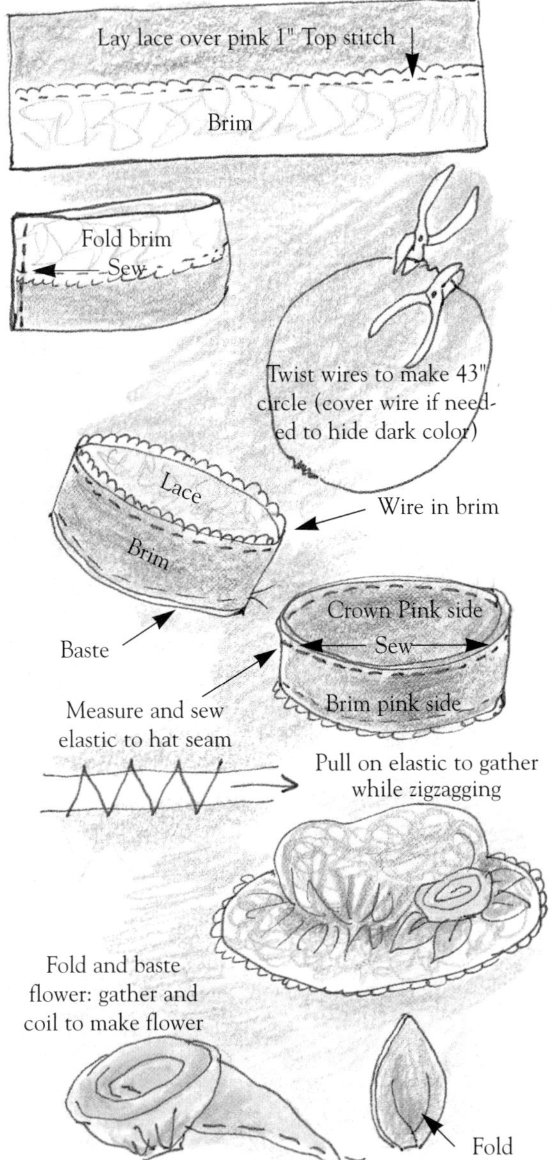

Project 23: Leslie's Banners

Medieval castles used banners and wall hangings to keep out drafts, warm a space visually, and as decoration. Furthermore, these fabrics were portable and went with the royal entourage when it moved about. Also, nomads have always used tents, rugs, and wall hangings to create living spaces. Banners provide the same service these days, even if the space is outside.

These banners were painted by Leslie Masters, long-time friend and fellow artist. Below she describes how she made them.

Leslie Master's says about her banners painted on organdy, "My idea was fields of flowers shaded from the lightest yellows at the top down to reds, greens, and blues below."

You need:

- *White cotton organdy. 2 yards*
- *Rod. 1/4″ dowel, 36″ long*
- *White thread*
- *Acrylic artist's paint and brushes*
- *Tools: water pail*

Making the pattern: Determine the banner size. Here the full width would be too hard to handle. This is the true size: 34″ x 63″. Hem both sides and across the bottom. Fold a top 2″ hem or one that will accommodate your rod. Use a 1/4″ wooden dowel or curtain rod because the fabric is lightweight.

Leslie describes how she painted these: "The 100 percent cotton organdy will take paint. I put down a flannel sheet on the tabletop to paint on, so anything that went through the open weave would continue through and not clog holes. My round hog-bristle, fairly stiff, brush made the paint penetrate the cloth. I drew the flowers with the brush first, then painted pale colors. The light colors need white for opacity to show up. I kept working through medium colors to bright and darker ones. These wet colors tend to spread softly. If you make a mistake, spray it with water, sop up the wet with a sponge or paper towels, and pat dry. This dries fast and is a permanent color."

Chapter 7

Sewing for Your Pergola

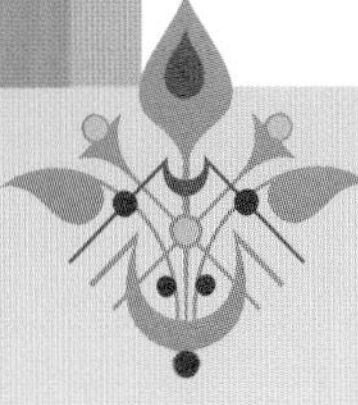

Photographed at Carol Chadwick's Pergola

Victoriana is about nostalgia for more romantic times. My memories aren't of castles and kings but picnics and gardens. My neighbor Carol Chadwick has created a charming bower for a tea party or contemplation. Here are playful projects designed for her wisteria-draped pergola.

Coordinated Martha Stewart fabrics plus a collection of waverly and other glazed chintzes create a Victorian ambiance under Carol Chadwick's pergola.

Project 24:

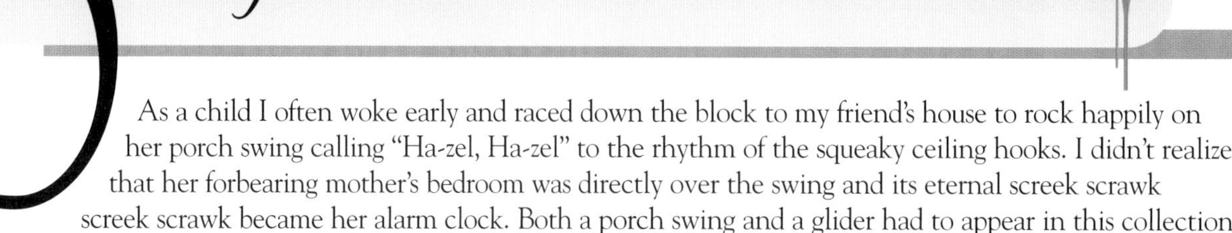

Swing cushion

As a child I often woke early and raced down the block to my friend's house to rock happily on her porch swing calling "Ha-zel, Ha-zel" to the rhythm of the squeaky ceiling hooks. I didn't realize that her forbearing mother's bedroom was directly over the swing and its eternal screek scrawk screek scrawk became her alarm clock. Both a porch swing and a glider had to appear in this collection of outdoor pleasures. This one is done Victorian style with lots of chintz and patchwork, ruffles and bows.

Carol's porch swing makes a cozy place to curl up with a good book—a romance novel, no doubt.

You need:

White background flower print. 30″ x 20″
Pink background flower print. 8″ x 36″
Dark green print. 11″ x 24″
White and green baroque print. 8″ x 24″
Pink background flower print. 30″ x 20″
Dark pink plain. 20″ x 20″
Dark green small print. 14″ x 20″
Light green background flower print. 13″ x 39″
Light green background/blue green plaid chintz. 96″ x 44″

Note: *Measure fabric needed from pattern pieces. Extra will be needed for centering design elements.*
Quilt bat of polyfill
Blue-green thread
Off-white thread
Tools: scissors, rotary cutter, metal yardstick, pencil, quilting pins

ABOUT FABRICS: The coordinated Martha Stewart pastel flower print and matching plaid combined with other chintz decorator fabrics and ribbons create the summery look of bygone days, yet this frothy style seems to be ever appealing. With a plaid print design fabric you must measure and cut according to the print which may not correspond to a torn edge.

MAKING THE PATTERN: Enlarge the pattern given, or draw a pattern by measurement with the metal ruler, pencil, and paper. Make four templates for Block 1 and four for Block 2 as shown. (Templates do not include seam allowances; add them later.)
Ruffles: Cut four strips 6-1/2″ (or as the pattern repeat requires) x 44″
Backing: 40″ x 60″
Ties: Three strips 3″ x 44″

Sewing the cushion:

1 Cushion: Assemble the front quilt blocks according to the diagram letters:

A. Trace around the templates with a pencil on the fabric back for the seam line. Add 1/2″ seam allowance. Cut out the pieces very accurately if you plan to serge them. By sewing machine, sew on the drawn seam lines for accuracy.

B. For Block 1, join A to B, B to C, and C to D for each of the four sections. Press seams in one direction. Pin two sections together, matching the seam lines, and sew. Repeat. Match the double sections, pin, and seam. Make three of Block 1.

C. For Block 2, the center square has no seams. Join F to E. Join F to the opposite edge. Join a longer F to both E edges. Join G to opposite F edges, join G to both remaining F edges. Join H to each G edge as shown. Press seams.

D. Cushion Seat: Join long pink I to opposite sides of Block 1. Join a Block 2 to each pink I.

E. Cushion Back: Join long I to opposite sides of Block 2. Join a Block 1 to each I.

F. Whole cushion: Match the seams of the three joined blocks 2, 1, 2 with 1, 2, 1 and sew.

2 Ruffle: Match the stripe patterns on the ends and join into one long strip. Use blue-green thread to serge a rolled hem in the entire piece. Set the serger differential feed to gather the fabric or gather by pulled thread. For more gather, run it through the serger again.

3 Ties: Fold both edges lengthwise and fold again to conceal the raw edges. Topstitch. Repeat for three ties. Clip each tie in two.

4 Assemble the cushion: Pin and baste the ruffle to the cushion front. Fold ties and pin one at each corner and the two side seams, ties tucked in. Baste the ties on. Pin the cushion back to the cushion front, ruffle and ties tucked in. For serging, place pins at least 2″ from the seam line into the fabric so there's no chance of sewing on a pin. Serge or sew all around, leaving an opening to turn 12″ long. Turn right-side-out.

5 Fold the quilt bat to make four layers. (Or two if this is too difficult for your sewing machine.) Cut the bat to fit (40″ x 60″) and tuck it into the cushion. Sew the opening closed. Use quilting pins to secure the layers and sew across the center seam. Zigzag in place (bartack) in block centers to quilt the layers.

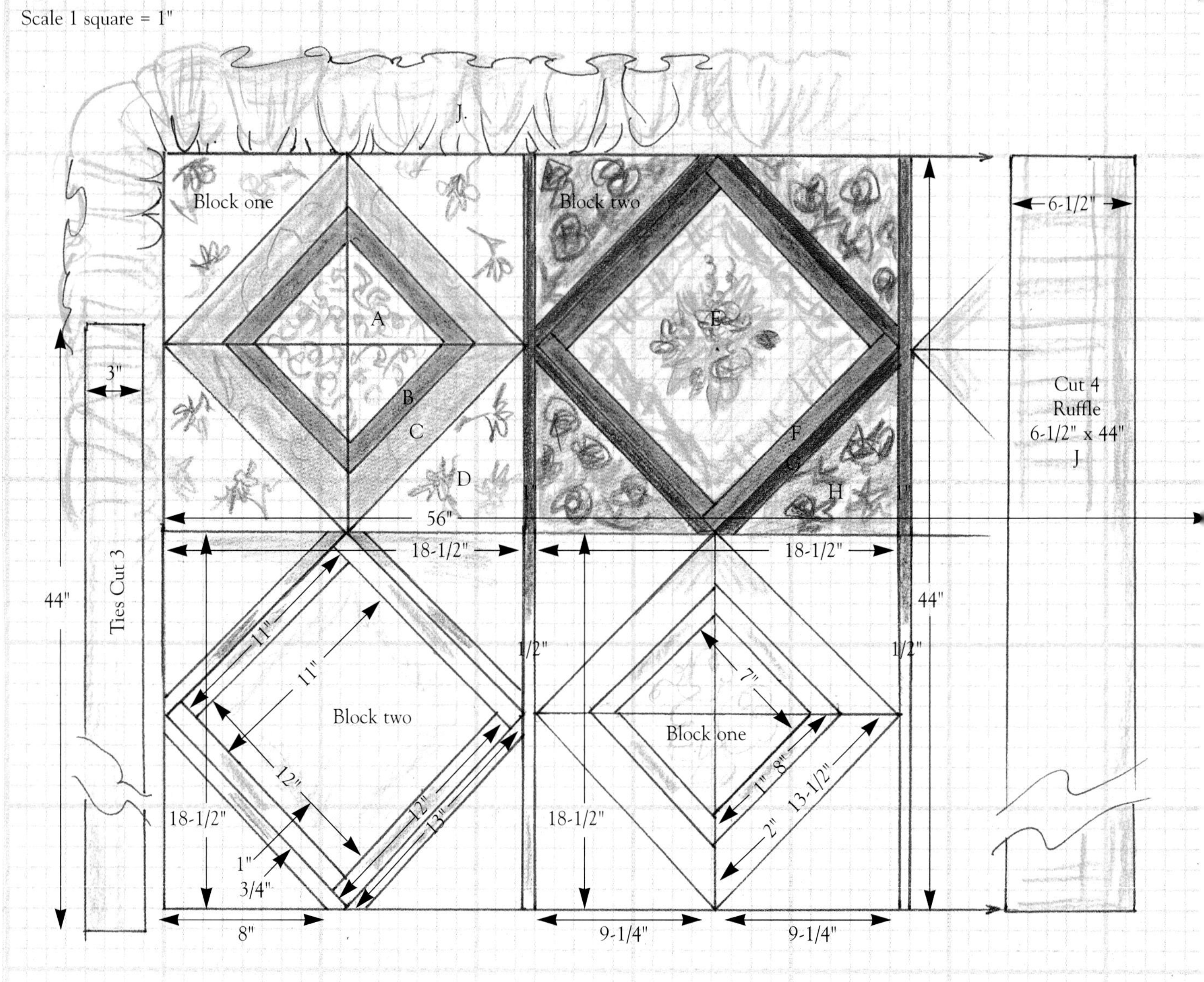

Scale 1 square = 1"
J.
Block one
Block two
A
B
C
D
E
F
G
H
1"
56"
18-1/2"
18-1/2"
44"
44"
Ties Cut 3
3"
6-1/2"
Cut 4
Ruffle
6-1/2" x 44"
J
1/2"
1/2"
11"
11"
12"
12"
13"
18-1/2"
1"
3/4"
8"
Block two
Block one
7"
8"
1"
13-1/2"
2"
18-1/2"
9-1/4"
9-1/4"

Block one
A
B
C
D
Make blocks from center out
Block 1
Join block and strings
1
2
Back of blocks
Sew
Leave open
Ruffle
Backing
Turn and insert stuffing
Pin in ruffle
and tuck in
Sew on ties
Sew
quilting
stitches
Bartack
centers to
quilt

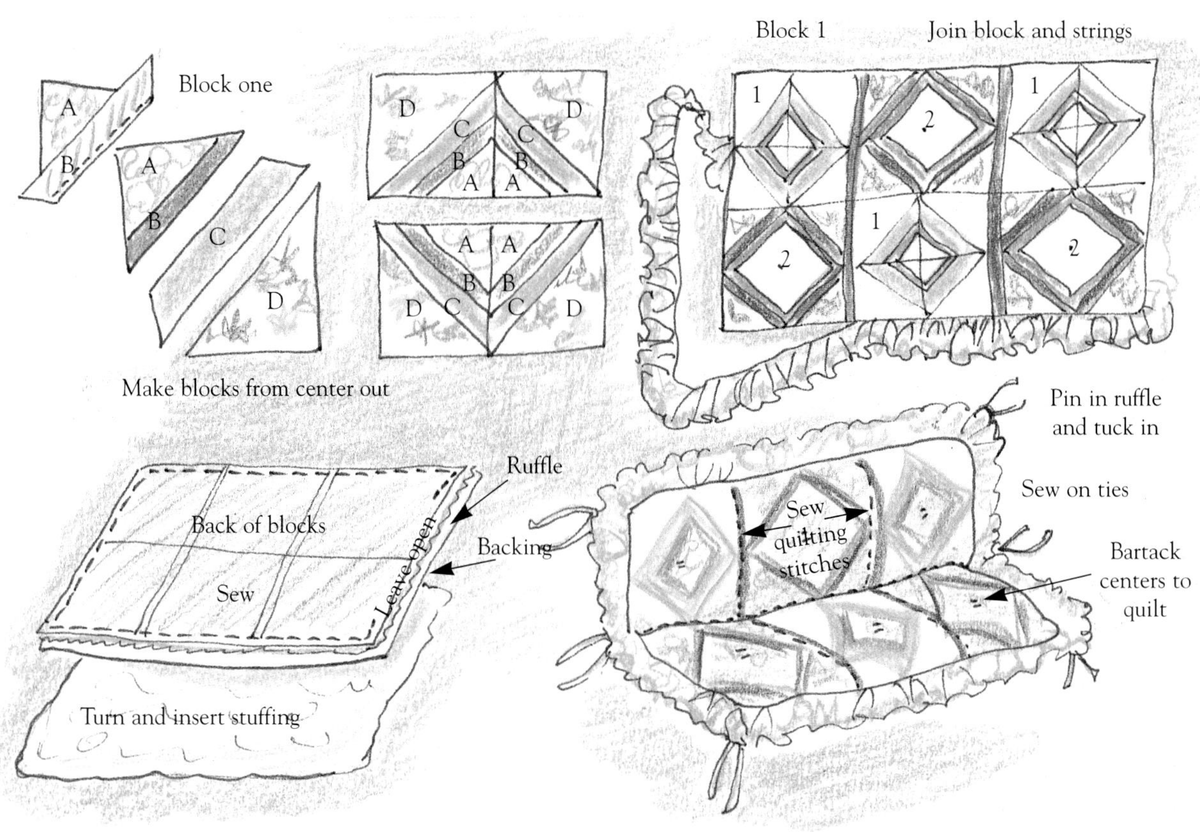

Project 25:

Wire basket

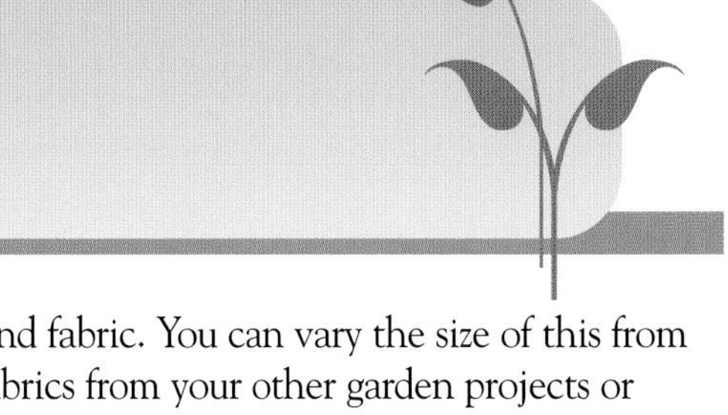

Here's an easy project made with garden fencing and fabric. You can vary the size of this from wastebasket to plant container size. Use matching fabrics from your other garden projects or choose anything from canvas to chintz.

Extra garden fencing provides a light-weight framework for this ruffled fabric basket.

You need:

Section of decorative wire fencing. 32″ long x 15″ high
Chintz or canvas. 1 yard
Ruffle. 1 yard (to make your own, 1/3 yard 36″ fabric)
2″ wide decorative wire-edged ribbon. 2 yards
10″ plastic picnic plate
Cord. 1 yard
Tools: pliers with clipper blades, scissors, elastic threader

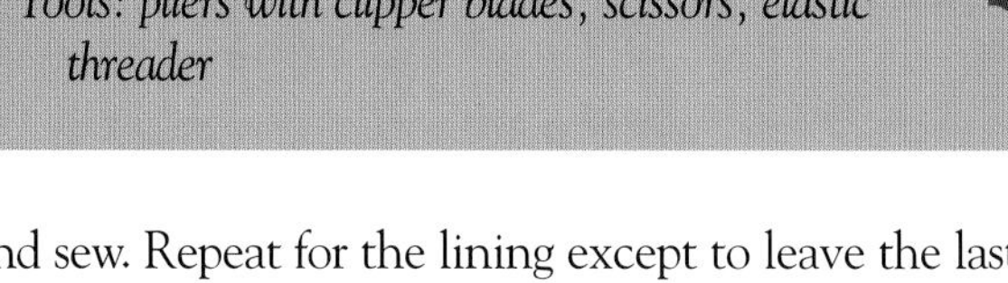

PATTERN: Clip off enough wire to surround plate plus overlap. A 10″ plate times 3.14 (pi) equals 32″ plus 3″ overlap. Cut two pieces of fabric 34″ x 16″. Cut two ruffle strips 36″ long x 5″ wide.

Making the basket:

1 Form the wire: Clip off extra wire so the fencing pattern fits neatly together. Bend the fencing into a circle so ends meet and overlap. Wrap the protruding ends around the matching wires by clamping the pliers over both pieces of wire side-by-side and twist. Fingers may work, but pliers will make a tighter twist. Bend the bottom wires inward to form the basket.

2 Sew the bag:

A. Sew the ruffle pieces end-to-end in a loop. Hem one edge and gather the other to fit the 32″ basket.

B. Lay the bag pieces face-to-face, 16″ side aligned, and sew. Repeat for the lining except to leave the last 2″ open. Hem this opening for the casing.

C. Align the ruffle to the bag top edge face-to-face and pin. Align the bag lining face-to-face with the ruffle and bag, pin, and sew. Turn the bag right-side-out.

D. Align the bottom edges and serge or sew a narrow hem. Topstitch around the bag, up 1-1/2″ from this to make the casing.

E. Insert the cord using the threader. Tie the cord in a granny knot and bow inside the bag so you can loosen or tighten gathering to make the bag shorter or longer.

F. Push the bag into the wire frame. Push the plate into the bag and down as far as it will go. Fold the ruffle and bag down over the basket sides. Tie the ribbon around the top of the bag and make a decorative bow. Weave various ribbons around the wire basket as shown, or as you invent.

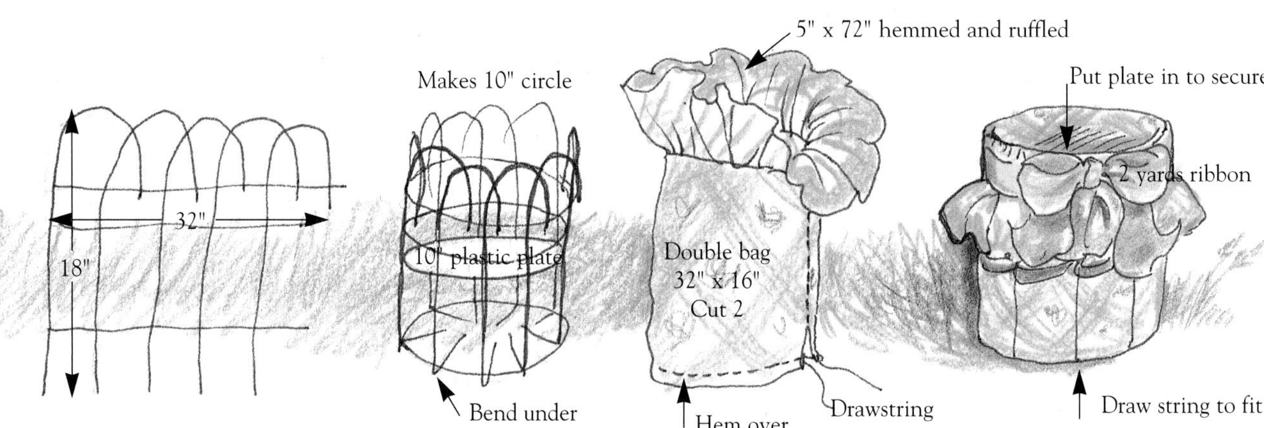

Project 26:

Layered tablecloths

The same coordinated flower print and matching plaid used for the swing cushion and basket are used here, plus a glitzy gold metallic fabric in between.

Carol layered tablecloths embellished with tassels, trim, and inch-wide welting for a Period look.

You need:

All fabric amounts and sizes are dependent on your table size.

To find your tablecloth size:

1. *For the top and middle square cloths (One and Two) measure across the tabletop. For the drop, measure down the side as far as you want the shortest hem to hang. Add the diameter of the table (across) and twice the drop plus two hem allowances. A square of this dimension makes a cloth with an uneven hem line (called a handkerchief hemline). Measure one side times four for trim amounts.*
2. *The underskirt tablecloth (Three) is round.*
   A. To determine the size you need, measure across the tabletop. Measure the drop to the floor. Add the diameter plus twice the drop, plus two seam allowances, to get the diameter. Decorator fabrics often come 60˝ wide, which allows cutting an unseamed circle. A seamed cloth will take almost twice as much fabric (or more) depending on matching the design repeats.
   B. For the welting fabric amount, multiply the cloth diameter (width determined above) by 3.14 to get the circumference. Cut this length strips wide enough to cover the welting cord.

Tools: thread, scissors, iron, ruler or tape, thumbtack, string, pencil, paper

Making the patterns and tablecloths:

❶ Tablecloths One and Two: No need to make a pattern for a hemmed square. Measure and cut to size by squaring the fabric or by the fabric print design, adding hem allowances. Make a rolled hem or hand press a hem and stitch. Add trim of your choice, like tassels, ribbons, or a braid.

❷ Tablecloth Three:

A. To make your pattern, draw a quarter circle the needed diameter. (See Project 12 for making a circle, page 36.) Fold fabric in quarters, measure out the radius distance from center, and draw the circle.

B. Fabric is flexible, some more than others, and will hang lower on the bias. Iron your cloth, put it on your table, and trim the cloth to the floor.

C. Make the welting: Join the welting cord strips at the ends into one long strip. Fold the strip over the welting cord and use a zipper foot to sew close to the cord. Leave the first and last 6 inches open.

D. Join the welting: Pin the welting seam allowance to the tablecloth at the floor length or 1˝ up. Remove pins at the ends, clip off, and join the welting ends. Join the cord ends. Fold the welting over the cord and sew. Re-pin the welting to the tablecloth and sew all around.

Project 27:

Flower pillow

The rose metallic fabric for this pillow provides contrast and highlight to the busy design of the swing cushion. This pillow cover's metallic fabric is washable with a back opening for removal.

You need:

44″ wide rose metallic lamé (for ruffle). 1 yard
Dark green brocade (for pillow backing). 11″ x 17″
Canvas (for pillow base). 10″
Peach metallic lamé (for pillow center). 8″ square
Fiberfill stuffing
Tools: thread, sharp scissors, pencil compass, sewing needle

PATTERN: Ruffle: cut five strips of rose metallic fabric 7″ x 44″ (or width of fabric). Use the compass to draw these circles: center 8″ gold metallic, center filler 4″ foam, base 11″ canvas. Cut out these circles.

Making the pillow:

1. To create a spiral stitch line on the canvas base, draw a 10″ diameter circle seam line (1/2″ seam allowances). Draw a compass arc from the 10″ circle to a 9″ circle, another from 9″ to an 8″ circle, and so on to the 4″ circle.
2. Ruffle: Match and sew the ends of the five strips to make one strip 6 yards. Fold the strips lengthwise face-side-out. From one end, taper the edges for 30″ from the fold to the raw edges. Gather the edges. Gather twice for more fullness.
3. Sew the ruffle to the canvas:

   A. Begin at the 10″ circle seam line. Pin the tapered ruffle end to the stitch line, ruffle outward, gathered edge over the seam line.

   B. Topstitch the ruffle's gathered edge to the spiral stitch line. Continue sewing the ruffle to the line all the way to the 4″ circle. Three inches before the end, tuck the end of the ruffle in over the stitch line to hide the raw edges. If the ruffle does not lie flat, push more gathering into the ruffle as you sew.

   C. Cover the raw edges: Begin where the ruffle completes the first circle. Smooth the ruffle flat and topstitch through it on the underlying seam line where it is sewn to the canvas. Continue to the center. Swerve over to the center line before the end of the ruffle.
4. Make the center: Run gathering stitches around the center fabric. Cut out the 4″ center filler 1/2″ thick. Tighten the gathering stitches to make the center fit smoothly over the stuffing. Sew the center onto the 4″ circle over the ruffle raw edges. Do this by hand-sewn hidden stitches or use the blind hem machine stitch.
5. Join the backing: Sew 1/2″ double hems on each straight side of the backing. Overlap the backing edges until it makes an 11″ circle and put two pins in this overlap to secure it. Tuck the ruffle inward and pin the backing seam line to the canvas seam line and stitch all around.
6. Finish the pillow: Remove the two pins in the overlapped backing. Turn the pillow right-side-out. Fill with stuffing through the opening and pat into shape.

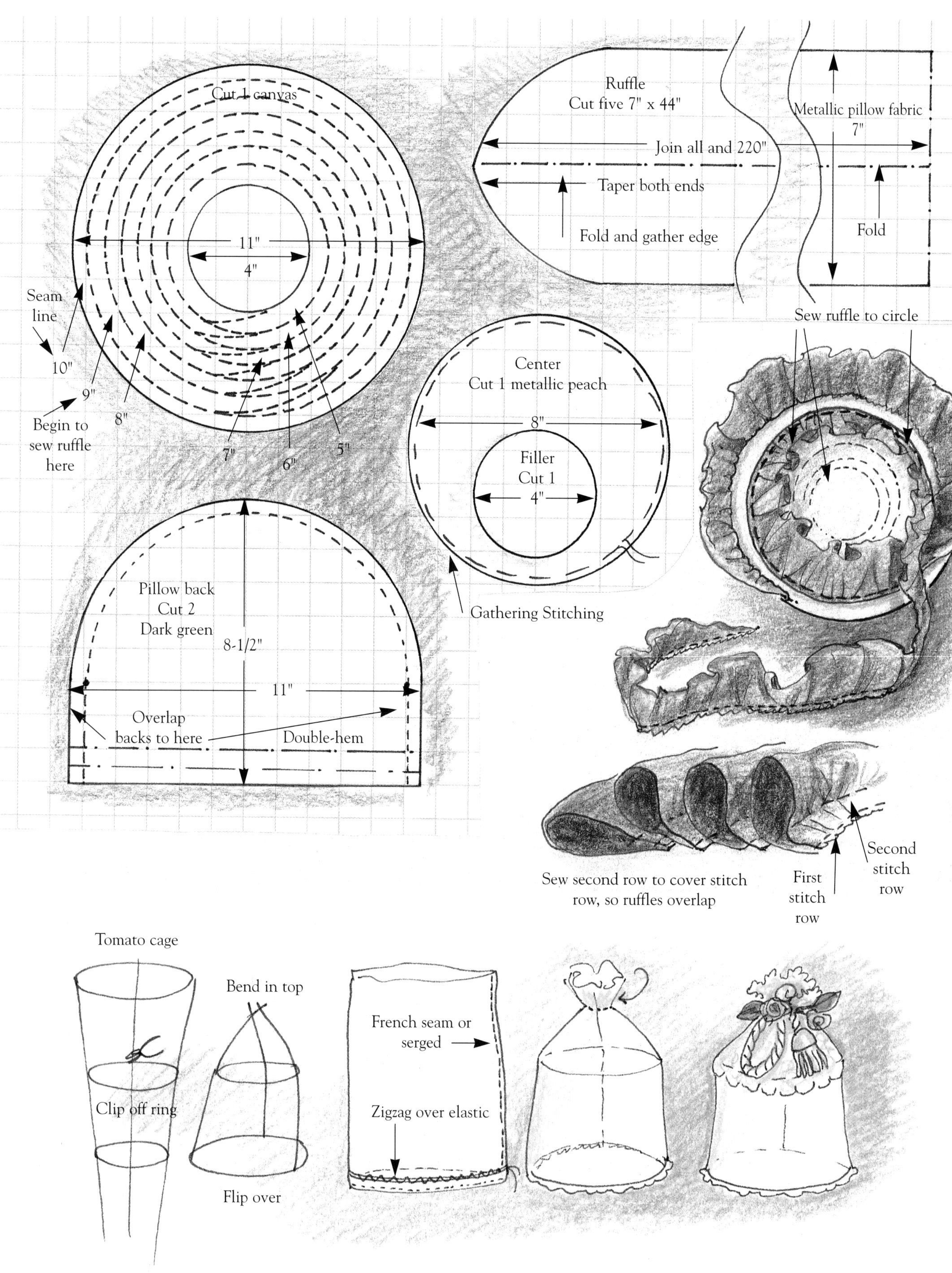

Cut 1 canvas
11"
4"
Seam line
10"
9"
Begin to sew ruffle here
8"
7"
6"
5"
Ruffle
Cut five 7" x 44"
Metallic pillow fabric
7"
Join all and 220"
Taper both ends
Fold and gather edge
Fold
Sew ruffle to circle
Center
Cut 1 metallic peach
8"
Filler
Cut 1
4"
Gathering Stitching
Pillow back
Cut 2
Dark green
8-1/2"
11"
Overlap
backs to here
Double-hem
Sew second row to cover stitch row, so ruffles overlap
First stitch row
Second stitch row
Tomato cage
Clip off ring
Bend in top
Flip over
French seam or serged
Zigzag over elastic

Project 28:

Food cover

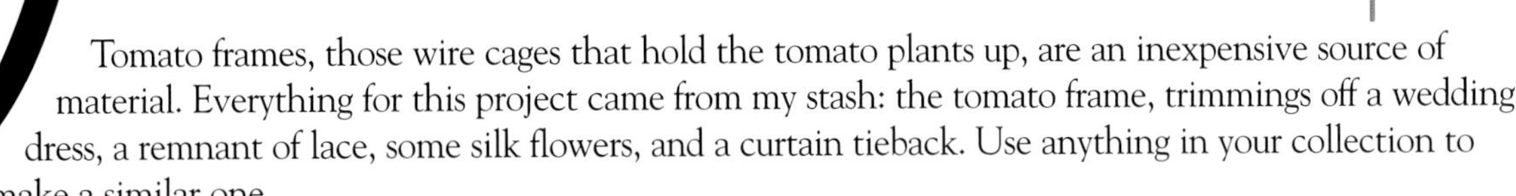

Tomato frames, those wire cages that hold the tomato plants up, are an inexpensive source of material. Everything for this project came from my stash: the tomato frame, trimmings off a wedding dress, a remnant of lace, some silk flowers, and a curtain tieback. Use anything in your collection to make a similar one.

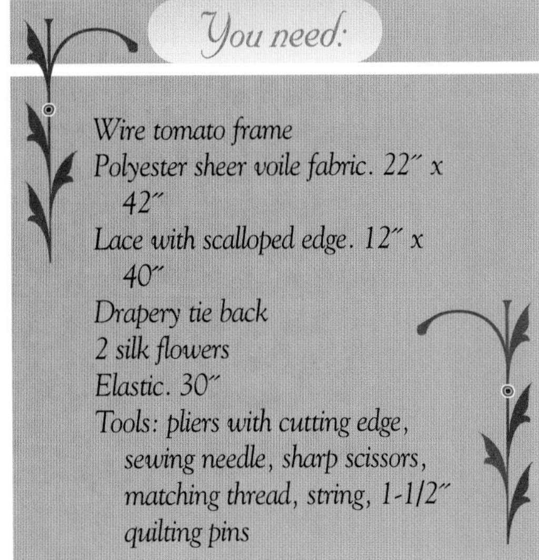

You need:

Wire tomato frame
Polyester sheer voile fabric. 22″ x 42″
Lace with scalloped edge. 12″ x 40″
Drapery tie back
2 silk flowers
Elastic. 30″
Tools: pliers with cutting edge, sewing needle, sharp scissors, matching thread, string, 1-1/2″ quilting pins

Such disparate materials as a tomato frame, wedding dress trimmings, and a drapery tie-back make up this sheer food cover.

Making the food cover:

1. Clip off the wire frame just below the middle ring. To do this, twist the pliers back and forth to make a groove, then bend to break. Bend the end wires inward to meet and cross by 1″. Wrap cord around this tightly to secure.
2. Wrap the voile around the slightly tapered frame and pin the fabric ends to determine the seam line. Make a narrow finished seam. I used the rolled hem on the serger. Serge a rolled hem around the tube base.
3. Align the elastic 3/4″ from the hem on the inside of the tube and zigzag (wide long stitch) over the elastic all around the tube. Put the tube on the frame and pull the elastic to tighten. With needle and thread, run a stitch line around the voile tube at the top, pull upward to fit the elastic with the lower edge. Pull the thread tight and sew. Twist the voile gathered ends at the top into a loop, pin to secure, and sew or tie in place.
4. Overcast-stitch the base wire and the elastic all around. (With a less flimsy fabric you could skip this step and make the cover removable.)
5. Wrap the lace, aligning its scalloped edge down 1-1/2″ from the top ring to measure for length. Sew a rolled hem seam up this edge to make a lace tube. Serge or hem the top edge of the lace. Fit the lace to the frame. Sew through the voile and the lace at the frame joinings to secure. Run a stitch line on the lace at the frame top, pull to gather, and sew to secure.
6. Thread a string through the large bead on the tie-back. Make the tie loops even and as long as possible. Tie one end of the string around the loops tightly and knot it to secure the loops. Repeat at the other side. Pull the string ends around the frame top, loop around twice, and tie tightly to secure.
7. Clip off the silk flower wire ends at 4″ and push the ends into the large tieback bead.

Chapter 8

Sewing for a Holiday Party

Photographed on Doug and Claudia Stroud's Patio

Windsocks, soft-sculpture garden figures, and banners celebrate the holidays. Here's a Fourth of July collection that you can make. Alter these ideas and techniques to fit other holidays.

It's 4th of July party time in the Stroud's garden with a red, white, and blue tablecloth, painted napkins, napkin rings, rocket windsock, and Uncle Sam.

Rocket windsock

Wire hoops help maintain the rocket shape, rain or shine. Make your own from florist's wire. The rocket and streamers are made of polyester flag cloth, a stiff nylon fabric, or heavy-weight polyester fabric. Sparkling touches come from squeeze tube puffy fabric paint.

This nylon rocket-shaped windsock with wire hoops and sparkling tails can't set anything afire!

You need:

Rocket body and top: 19″ x 30″ red polyester fabric
Streamers: Seven strips 2″ x 44″ for two white, two gold, four blue streamers
2 wires. 18″
Red and gold sparkle squeeze puff paint
Threads. Red, blue, and white
Tools: zipper foot

MAKING THE PATTERN: Rocket body 19″ x 25″ (measure and cut darts as shown), rocket tab 2″ x 4″, streamers cut 2″ wide strips and taper each to 1/2″ at one end

Sewing the object:

1 Squeeze paint fireworks and stars on the rocket body and streamers, staying clear of seam lines. You can do this after construction, but it's messier.

2 Tab: Fold a 1/2″ hem in the edges lengthwise, fold again, and topstitch.

3 Streamers: Serge, overcast, or make a rolled hem in all edges.

4 Rocket body:

A. Fold the body to align side edges and serge, seam, and overcast, or French seam up 19″ to finish this edge.

B. Fold the top 6″ into the rocket, pin or press, and sew a 1/4″ casing for the wire. Leave 1/4″ open to insert wire.

C. To shape the top, still wrong-side-out, align and sew the four darts. Fold the tab, push the ends into the top's tip, and sew. Bend the wire in a circle and insert. Turn right-side-out.

5 Assembly: Align the top of each streamer to the body face-to-face and machine baste in place. Fold a double 1/2″ hem (including the streamers) in the body and topstitch. Bend the wire into a hoop and insert behind streamers.

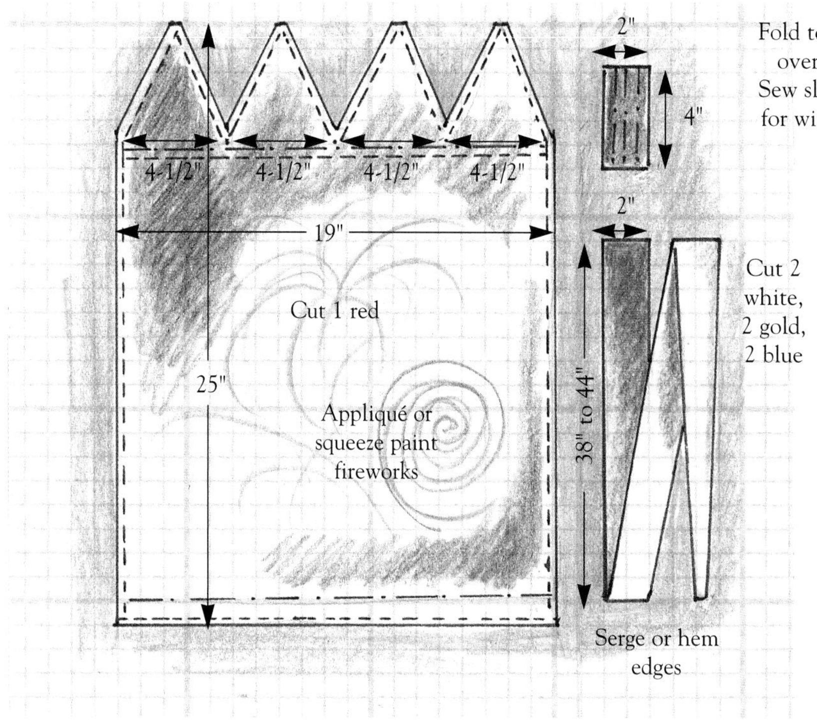

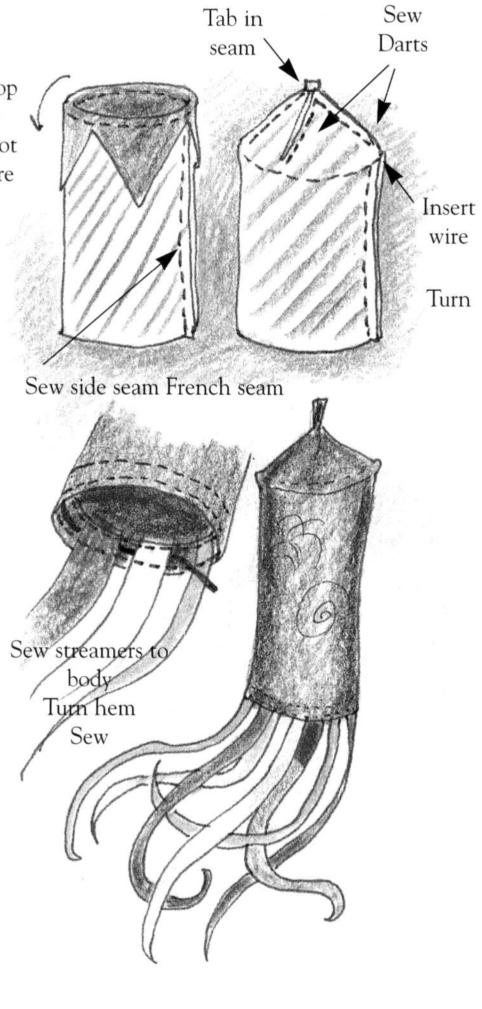

Project 30:

Uncle Sam

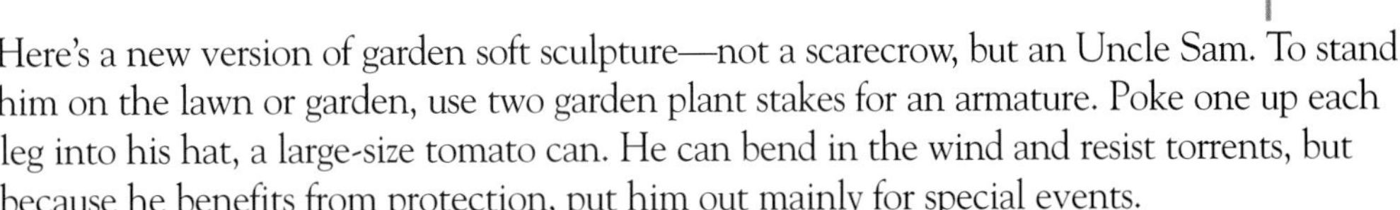

Here's a new version of garden soft sculpture—not a scarecrow, but an Uncle Sam. To stand him on the lawn or garden, use two garden plant stakes for an armature. Poke one up each leg into his hat, a large-size tomato can. He can bend in the wind and resist torrents, but because he benefits from protection, put him out mainly for special events.

You need:

- Flag cloth
  - Blue 1 yard x 44″
  - Red 1/2 yard x 44″
  - White-1/2 yard x 44″
  - Flesh 6″ x 9″
- Felt. 5″ x 6″
- Quilted gold metallic fabric. 6″ x 44″
- 2 button eyes
- 2 plant stakes. 6' (each)
- Empty tomato can. 4″ diameter x 4-3/4″ tall
- White and blue thread
- Long, stiff wire. 2 pieces, 18″ each
- Tools: sharp scissors, ruler, pattern paper, compass

Uncle Sam, made in flag cloth and gold metallic fabric with a tomato can hat and black button eyes, can stand on the lawn or in the garden with his plant-stake legs.

ABOUT FABRICS: Flag fabrics, nylon, and polyester, are coupled with a quilted metallic fabric.

MAKING THE PATTERN: (See page 77) Pattern pieces are given full size for the face 4-1/2″ x 3″ (cut two, one reversed), chin 2-3/4″ x 3-1/4″, mouth 2-3/4″ x 2″, beard 2-1/2″ x 4-1/2″, eyebrows 5″ x 2″, all including 1/4″ seam allowances. Felt hands 2-1/2″ x 4-1/4″ (cut two, one reversed), no seam allowances.
The other simpler pieces can be scaled or measure to size from the diagram. These include 1/2″ seam allowances. Pattern pieces include hat stripe 1-1/2″ x 5-3/4″ (cut seven red, six white), hat band 1-1/2″ x 13″, top 5″ circle, brim 6-1/2″ circle (cut two), hair 5-1/2″ x 8-1/2″, collar 2″ x 13-1/2″, shirt 10″ x 2-1/2″, lapel 10″ x 3-3/4″ triangle (cut two, one reversed), jacket front 6-1/2″ x 12″ (cut two, one reversed), jacket back 12″ x 12″, sleeve 18″ x 7″ (cut two), coat tails 9″ x 14″ (cut two), pants stripes 1-1/2″ x 28″ (cut twelve red, twelve white). Cut out all pieces.

Sewing Sam:

(See page 78)

❶ Hat: Make the hat to fit the empty can, 4-3/4″ tall x 12-1/2″ around x 4″ across the top.

A. Alternate sewing a red to a white stripe until the hat piece measures 13-1/2″ across by 5-3/4″ tall. Match and sew the hat band across the stripes. Fit the hat/band to the can, seams out, and pin a side seam. Remove, sew the side seam, and refit to the can, seam side out.

B. Pin the top to the hat. Remove can and sew. (Put a tab in this seam if you plan to hang him instead.)

C. Align the brims and sew around the edge with 1/4″ seam allowances. Turn right-side-out. Trace the can top on the brim for the cut out, add 1/4″ seam allowance inside circle.

❷ Face: Assemble the pieces.

A. Fold the mouth, place it fold-up on the chin, and topstitch. Fold the mouth down and seam across the center to make lips. Fold lips up and pin.

B. Fold the beard, sew, and turn. Place the beard's raw ends on the chin, matching raw edges. Topstitch across.

C. Match the face pieces and sew from top to nose tip. Open. Fold the eyebrows and align on face, stitch across. Fold eyebrows down and stitch seam down the center. Sew on eyes.

D. Align assembled chin to the face face-to-face and sew. Clip the seam allowances at inside corners.

E. Match the hair with the face side and sew. Fit the head over the can and pin the face/hair seam for a loose fit. Sew.

F. Fold and seam the collar ends. Fit to the face/hair bottom face-to-face with the beard tucked upward and sew to join.

❸ Head:

A. Align hat band right-side-out with brim hole, pin, and sew.

B. Align hat/brim with face/hair face-to-face and sew. Clip seam allowances so hat fits over can. Bend the wire into an 18″ circle and insert the wire into the brim.

❹ Arms:

A. Fold cuff lengthwise. Fold cuff in half across. Align the hand top with the cuff's raw edges. Sew across cuff top and down raw ends. Clip corner seam allowance and turn cuff.

B. Fold sleeve end over the cuff fold-to-fold, raw edges aligned. Sew across the sleeve/cuff and up **half** the length of the sleeve. Clip the corner seam allowance. Repeat.

❺ Body:

A. Fold and sew coat tails, turn, and press. Match tails to the back of the coat face-to-face and seam across.

B. Coat front: Match the lapel to the coat front face-to-face. Seam the long edge, open flat, and topstitch the lapel. Repeat. Align the lapel with the shirt triangle face-to-face and sew. Repeat. Open and press.

C. Join the coat back and front shoulder seams, sew, and overcast. Align the sleeve top center with the shoulder seam and sew. Repeat.

D. Tuck right-side-out head into body, align the collar with the coat neck hole, pin, and sew.

E. Align an 18″ wire with the shoulder/neck seam. Push the wire through the overcast stitching. Bend the wire ends in a 1-1/2″ loop for shoulder pads.

F. Match the coat front and back. Sew the side seam and continue down the sleeve to stitched seam. Repeat.

❻ Pants:

Stitch twelve alternating red and white stripes together. Repeat. Press with seam allowances to the red side. Fold pants stripes face-to-face lengthwise and sew the side seam to 6″ from the end for the crotch. Repeat. Turn up a 1/2″ double hem in each pant leg and sew. Align crotch seams and sew. Serge a finished edge all around the pants top.

❼ Finish the figure:

A. Align the coat lower edge with the pants upper edge face-to-face with the tails tucked up. Begin to sew 2″ from the side seam toward the front, across the front to 2″ into the coat back, leave an opening to turn. Turn right-side-out and sew opening closed. Fold a tuck in the pants/coat front at the pants crease line from a red to a red stripe and stitch from the back side to hold.

B. Insert a plant stake up each leg into the tomato can. The stakes will cross in the head. Push stakes into the ground.

ale 1 square = 1"   Add 1/4" seam allowances to all

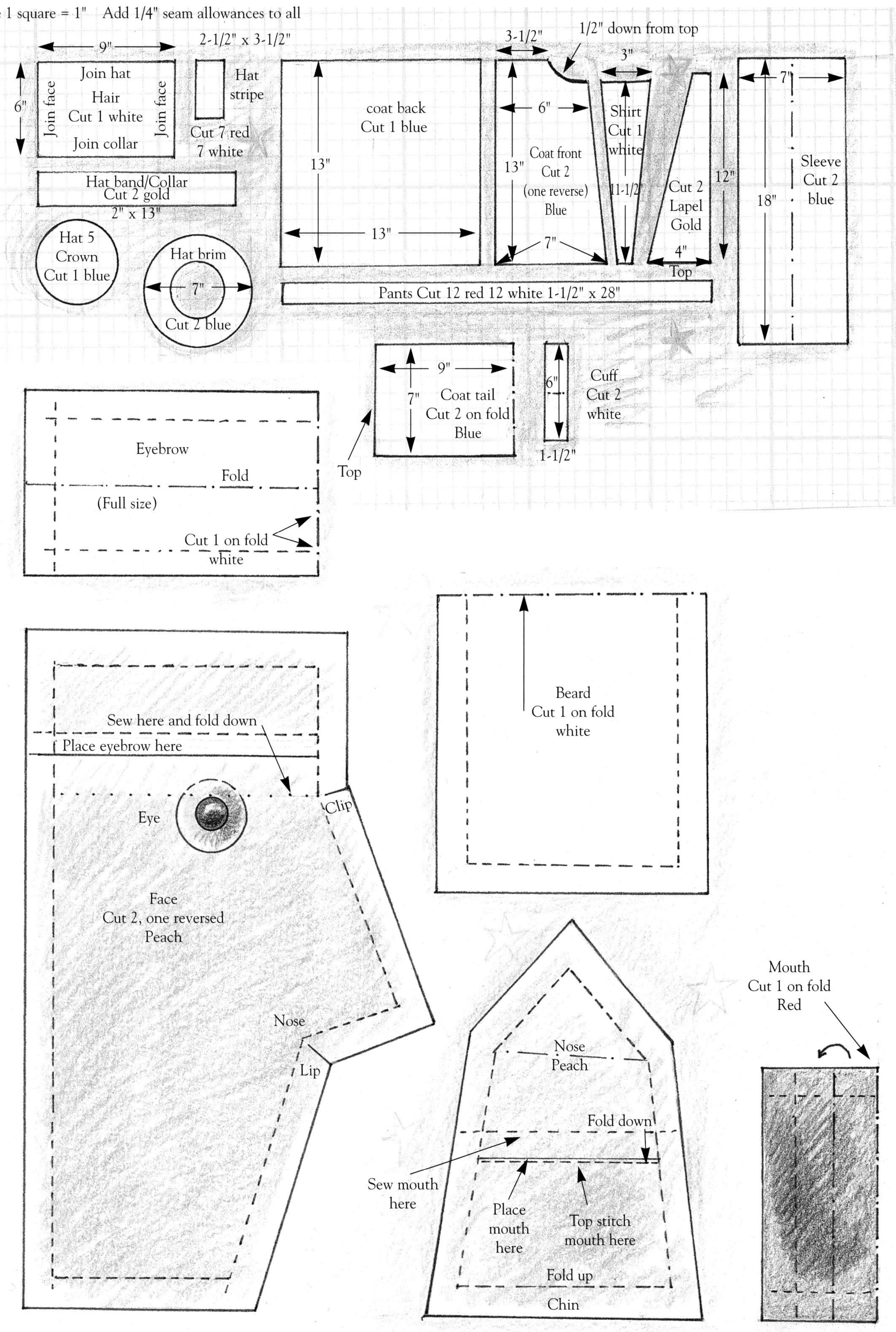

1
A
B
C
2
A
B
C
D
E
3
A
B
4
A
B
5
A
B
C
D
E
F
A
B
6
7

Project 31:

Tablecloth

This quilted tablecloth began life some years ago as a holiday tablecloth. With the addition of a slit to a center hole it became a Christmas tree skirt and now it is an outdoor tablecloth with an umbrella hole.

Traditional colors on this patched tablecloth are tweaked a bit for subtlety: blue to navy, red to red-orange, and white to eggshell.

You need:

Navy blue quilt print. 4-1/2 yards
Navy poly-cotton. 24″ x 22″
Pre-quilted lining. 4 yards (at least 36″ wide)
Red double-fold bias tape. 8 yards
Navy thread
Tools: yardstick, paper for pattern, scissors

FABRICS: Quilting cotton and poly-cotton fabrics have maintained their colors well through use and washing. The eyelet border matches the pre-quilted cotton and fiberfill lining fabric.

MAKING THE PATTERN: Enlarge or scale up the pattern. Add 1/2″ seam allowances. One eighth of the pattern has three pattern pieces: center diamond, border, and triangle. Cut these pieces: sixteen diamond patterned fabric, sixteen borders navy, sixteen triangle patterned fabric. Use bias tape or cut sixteen strips 1-1/2″ wide (total 8 yards). For the backing, make a 72″ circle as described on page 36.

Sewing the tablecloth:

1 Assemble the patchwork top. Press seam allowances to the side as you sew the seams.

A. Align the border outside edge face-to-face with the triangle inside edge and seam. Repeat for all sixteen border/triangle pieces.

B. Bias: For home-cut strips, fold and press the strips. Align the tape or strips with the top edge of the navy border faceup. Pin or machine baste in place.

C. Align the border/triangle plus bias with the outside edge of the star face-to-face and sew. Repeat for all sixteen diamonds. Align the diamond long edges face-to-face and seam. Repeat for all sixteen diamonds.

D. Align two completed pieces face-to-face and edge-to-edge, pin, and seam. Repeat eight times. Align two doubled pieces face-to-face and seam. Repeat. Join the two halves of the cloth face-to-face along the straight seam.

NOTE: See Project 20, page 56, as an example of assembly.

2 Join the two halves of the quilted backing face-to-face and sew, leaving a 12″ opening to turn in the center of the seam.

3 Assemble the tablecloth:

A. Align the eyelet edge with the pieced top edge and pin or machine baste. Join the eyelet ends and seam. Do not unfold the eyelet.

B. Match the top with the backing and pin across the seam line all around the edge. Sew this seam including the eyelet edge. Turn the cloth right-side-out through the backing seam opening.

C. Pull on the eyelet to flatten the edges. Topstitch 1/2″ from the edge all around to quilt the top to the backing. Topstitch in the ditch along the star seam lines to quilt the top.

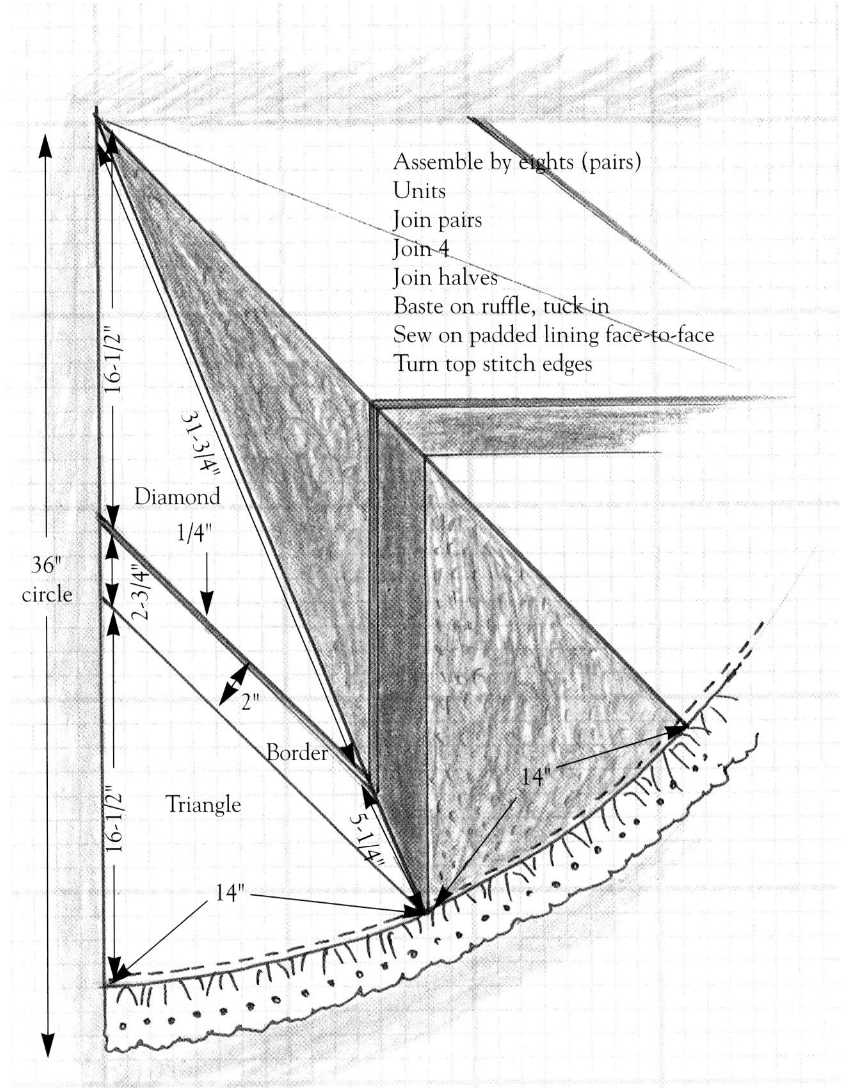

Project 32:

Napkins & rings

"Hattie, we need an easy project," I said, and my granddaughter quickly created these napkin rings and suggested the squeeze paint napkins. They add a festive air to the holiday. Red, white, or blue napkins carry out the patriotic theme. For the napkins use no-iron poly-cotton, because you cannot iron over the paint later. For the rings use red, white, and blue felt.

You need:

Navy blue poly-cotton fabric (for the napkins). 30" x 45" (15" square for each)
Puffy glitter fabric paint in red, gold, purple, green, gold
White thread (woolly nylon serger thread makes a nice edge)
Red, white, and blue felt (for the napkin rings). 1-1/2" x 6" (each color) (each ring takes three strips of felt)
Glitter pipe cleaners in gold, red, or blue. 2 for each ring
Tools: sharp scissors or rotary cutter, ruler

RIGHT: Sparkle fabric paint squeezed on in swooping shapes created these colorful fireworks.

LEFT: Hattie Stroud braided felt strips for napkin rings and covered the joining string with metallic-colored pipe cleaners.

Making the pattern and sewing the pieces:

❶ Napkins: Cut six pieces 15˝ square. To finish the edges, serge, make a rolled hem, or turn a narrow double hem. Press. Lay the napkins flat and decorate with squeeze puffy fabric paint. Fireworks are easy to do.

❷ Napkin rings: Fold double hems in the strips lengthwise and fold again to tuck in the edges. Topstitch or plan to hold the folds as you braid. Pin the pieces together at one end. Braid the strips. Hand or machine sew across the ends. Make a loop and hand sew the ends together. Wrap the pipe cleaners around the joining.

Chapter 9

Sewing for Your Tailgate Party

Photographed at Garrett and Joan Hall's Tailgate Party

Garrett and Joan Hall, avid University of Michigan fans, have created a room-to-go with the Delt Party Hut tent. Making your own tent is possible, especially with the lighter weight nylons and other synthetic fabrics available, but it's still a hassle with yards of fabric and the need for sturdy demountable supports. Do as the Halls did and use a commercial pop-up tent to decorate. This tent stores in a compact 12″ square by 48″ long bag. These two can put it up like an umbrella in 5 minutes, but it's easier with a person on each corner.

Son Garrett Hall holds Joan Hall's gift to him, a Coach Schembechler autographed football, in their tailgate party hut.

Party hut tent banners

Garrett and Joan wanted the classic look of appliquéd satin-stitch outline letters for their banners on the tent—and were willing to do the work to make them. Garrett taped industrial-strength Velcro to the tent flaps to secure the weather-resistant polyester banners, which are then packed away, awaiting the next home game.

You need:

Blue (or school color) sport-weight fabric (for banners). 6 yards x 44″ for this 8′ x 8′ tent
Fabric in maize with white underlay (for lettering). 2 yards x 44″ each color
Iron-on fusible (HeatnBond). 5 yards
Tear-away stabilizer paper or scrap typing paper. 5 yards
Tools: sharp scissors, embroidery thread (blue and maize), yardstick, tape measure, backing paper, masking tape, 1-1/2″ quilting pins

ABOUT FABRICS: Try for fade-resistant acrylic, nylon, or polyester when buying fabrics for the tent banners. Note that light-colored fabrics, such as lettering over a dark color, will need a white lining layer for a clearer color.

MAKING THE PATTERN: Banners: 11″ x 96″ (each). Measure wherever you plan to hang the banners. Add 1″ for hems and a few inches more for the contraction of satin-stitching. Cut the blue fabric double 22″ x 8-1/2′.
Letter patterns: 7″ to 8″ high printed in outline on paper

Sewing the banners:

1 Fold the banner lengthwise to double it and sew around the edges, leaving an opening to turn. Turn and press. Topstitch edges with a double row.
2 Design the banner:
A. Choose a typeface consistent with the school logo, here a block M. Plan your lettering to fit the banner length. Garrett entered his text on computer, enlarged it to size (use the "other" font size), and printed one or two letters per page in outline form. Or, you can get lettering from an art supply store or print shop.
B. Make the letters: (To line light-colored letters,

LEFT: Joan holds the demountable sides used for wind, rain, and sun protection on those gusty University of Michigan football weekends.
ABOVE: Two people can put the tent up in 5 minutes, Garrett says "it's even quicker with four."
ABOVE RIGHT: Garrett uses industrial-strength Velcro to hang the appliquéd U of M banners that he, Joan, and mom sewed.

iron fusible on white lining, peel off backing, and iron onto the maize.) Trace the letter on fusible in reverse and iron the fusible to the (lined) maize back. Cut the letter out, but don't peel the fusible until you are ready to sew. Repeat for each letter.

C. Position the lettering: Peel the backing paper off. Spread out the banner and place the lettering. To center, count the letters and spaces between, divide in half, and place the center letter in the center of the banner. Measure carefully to place letters accurately.

D. Secure the letters with masking tape. (You can use an extension cord and towel backing to iron the banner spread on the floor.) Remove tape to iron the letters in place and replace the tape because constant handling in sewing can release the fusible.

E. On the banner back, add tear-away stabilizer behind each letter to diminish puckering and pin. Satin-stitch around each letter in matching or contrasting machine embroidery thread. Tear away the stabilizer.

F. Place a vertical strip of Velcro on each banner end. The adhesive back of heavy-weight industrial Velcro really sticks. Sewing-weight Velcro must be sewn on to hold.

PENNANTS: The pennants clamped to the upright poles are made in the same manner as the banner. Trace the image on HeatnBond in reverse, iron this to the fabric, cut out the shape, and peel the backing. Lay the pennant over the drawing to place the design accurately and iron in place. Satin-stitch around each shape with tear away stabilizer on the back. Sew a rod pocket on one end.

Project 34:

Chair backs

You need:

Frame
Canvas (for seat and back). 18″ x 49″ per chair and contrasting colors for the design
Blue and maize machine embroidery thread
1/4″ metal rods 16″ long. Need 2
Matching sewing thread
Tools: computerized sewing machine for lettering

ABOUT FABRICS: Canvas comes 60″ wide to accommodate tarps and tents of large sizes. One hundred percent cotton or poly canvases treated to repel water are best. A sling seat takes all the weight of a person and must be strong.

PATTERN: Seat finished size of 16-1/2″ x 19-1/2″, back finished size of 6-1/2″ x 19-1/2″. Cut one 18″ x 22″ maize, back 7-1/2″ x 29″ blue.

Maize and blue captains' chairs wear computer-sewn lettering on the backs. The pack-up tent, rolled party kit, plastic box for the banners, sides and pennants, as well as the folding chairs, all fit in their Ford convertible trunk.

Sewing the chair seats:

1. Apply seat decorations at this point. You can use fabric or acrylic paint, embroidery, or appliqué. What you use needs to withstand wear and tear.
2. Fold a double hem 1/2″ or less in the front and back of the seat. Sew across with matching thread. Serge across the seat side edges or turn a narrow hem 1/4″ or less. Turn again 1″ for a rod slot. (The seat should measure 19-1/2″ across or fit the frame you have.) Sew across this hem, leaving room for inserting the rod.
3. Back: Measure and cut the back 7-1/2″ x 29″. Decorate the back. The machine embroidery shown was done on a Brother PC 7000 that has computer settings for automatically sewing wonderful letters. If you guide your machine by hand, aim for a casual letter style or writing. Sew the lettering on an added piece to appliqué to the chair back so the reverse lettering will not show on the reverse side.

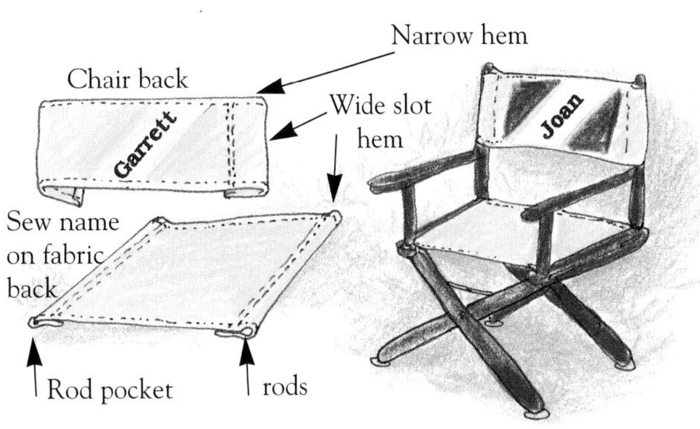

Project 35:

Party hut kit

"We need a way to keep track of all the stuff—plates, cutlery, cups," Garrett and Joan agreed. So this party kit was designed to hold everything, show clearly what was there, hang on the tent side, and then roll up to put away for the next home game.

About fabrics: The same heavy blue and maize canvas used for the chair seats appears here. A heavyweight clear vinyl makes sturdy pockets. It does stick on the presser foot or needle plate during sewing. Keep lifting the presser foot every few inches to release drag or use a Teflon presser foot.

For use, unroll the canvas shoe bag-style party kit and tie it to the tent. Vinyl pockets show what's where: cutlery, napkins, cups, a bottle opener, and more.

You need:

Blue canvas. 1 yard of 60″
Maize canvas. 24″ x 41″
Clear heavy-weight vinyl. 1 yard
Elastic. 36″
Blue thread
Heavy-weight plastic zipper (or Velcro strip). 24″
Tools: rotary cutter, sharp scissors, metal ruler, chalk pencil, elastic threader

PATTERN: Measure and cut these pieces. Blue canvas pieces: back 24″ x 41″, flaps 10″ x 14″ (two) with serged edges, binding for pockets 2-1/2″ x 129″ (cut into four: 25″, 28″, 32″, 44″), ties 1-1/2″ x 19″ (two) and 1-1/2″ x 35″ (two), binding for edges 2″ x 56″, handles 2″ x 12″ blue canvas (two) and vinyl (two), zipper tabs 2″ square (two).
Maize canvas: front 24″ x 41″
Clear vinyl: handles 2″ x 12″ (one or two), top pocket 10-1/2″ x 30″, second pocket 4-1/2″ x 24″, middle pocket 11-1/2″ x 32″, fourth pocket 4-1/2″ x 27″, bottom pocket 11-1/2″ x 44″.

Sewing the kit:

1 Ties: Double-fold lengthwise to cover raw edges and topstitch. Sew across at the ends to secure.

2 Handles: Match the vinyl and blue handles, double-fold with vinyl outside to cover raw edges, and topstitch.

A. On the blue back, measure up 13″ from the bottom, center the handle ends 4″ apart, and satin-stitch to join securely.

B. Match the maize front and blue back and machine baste around the edges.

C. On the maize front, measure down from the top 10″, 14″, 25″ and 29″. Use a chalk pencil (removable markings) to mark these lines across.

3 Make the Pockets:

A. Top pocket: Sew the zipper tabs to the ends of the zipper, face-to-face, and unfold.
Fold the tabs under the zipper on the bottom edge and pin. Align the zipper faceup on the vinyl. Fold a 1″ wide pleat in from the side and 1-1/2″ on each side of the 10-1/2″ x 30″ vinyl strip to make it 24″ wide. Align the zipper and tabs faceup on the top edge and topstitch it to the vinyl. Lay the vinyl strip face-to-face on the front below the top drawn mark, overlapping it 1/2″. Topstitch across. Use a Teflon presser foot, or keep lifting the presser foot every few inches to relieve drag. Fold the pocket up and align the zipper with the top edge. Pin and machine both sides.

B. Second pocket: Align the binding to the 4-1/2″ x 25″ vinyl pocket top edge and sew across with 1/2″ seam allowance. Fold a 1/2″ hem, fold again over the vinyl, and topstitch. Lay the pocket face-to-face below the second drawn mark, overlapping it 1/2″. Topstitch across. Unfold. Measure in from both edges 6″ and zigzag stitch up the pocket. Match the pocket to the front sides and baste both sides.

C. Middle pocket: Bind the 11-1/2″ x 32″ vinyl pocket top edge as above. Fold 1″ wide pleats in the vinyl at both side in 1″ and fold a pair of 1/2″ pleats in 6″ from the pleated sides. Lay the pocket face-to-face below the third drawn mark overlapping it 1/2″. Topstitch across. Unfold. Measure in from both edges 6″ and zigzag stitch between the 1/2″ pair of pleats up the pocket. Baste both sides.

D. Fourth pocket: Bind the 4-1/2″ x 27″ vinyl pocket top edge as above. Fold 1/2″ wide pleats in 4″ from each side and in the center. Lay the pocket face-to-face below the fourth mark, overlapping it 1/2″. Topstitch across. Unfold. Measure in from both edges 8″ and zigzag stitch up the pocket. Baste both sides.

E. Bottom pocket: Bind the 11-1/2″ x 36″ vinyl pocket top edge as above. Thread elastic into this binding slot, securing it at 6″ from the edge. Repeat for the other edge. Fold 1-1/4″ wide pleats in the vinyl at both sides in 1″ and fold a pair of 1-1/4″ pleats in 6″ from the pleated sides. Lay the pocket on the maize front and baste across the bottom. Measure in from both edges 6″ and zigzag stitch between the 1-1/4″ pair of pleats up the pocket. Pull the elastic in the binding tight. Match the pocket to the front and baste both sides securing the elastic in the seam.

4 Flaps: Serge or hem the edges of the flaps. Make two 1-1/2″ buttonholes, 1-1/2″ apart on the flap point and in 1-1/2″. Lay the flap on the blue kit back and align the edges 13″ down from the top edge. Repeat on the other side.

5 Bind the kit edges. Sew a strip 41″ long on each side face-to-face. Fold a narrow hem, then fold again over the edge, and topstitch in place. For the top and bottom edges fold a hem in each binding end to match the width. Join the binding, fold a narrow hem, then fold again over the edge, and topstitch in place.

6 Attach the end of one 19″ tie and one 25″ tie together, 4″ from each corner on the top binding. Zigzag stitch to reinforce. Join the handle centered on the top with the ends 4″ apart. Satin-stitch to reinforce and

cover the raw ends.

7 To use the kit, pack the pockets full, roll inward, folding at the sewn pocket lines. Pull the flaps over the rolled kit. Thread the long ties through the buttonholes, wrap them around the kit, and tie to the short ties. Tote the kit by the handles and use the ties to tie it to the party hut tent.

Top pocket
1"
1-1/2" wide
pleat in vinyl
Fold 1-1/2"
6"
zigzag stitch
6"
Fold kit here to roll
into bundle
1/2"
pleat
1/2"
pleat
1/2"
fold
1/2"
fold
1/2"
fold
1-1/4"
folds
1-1/4"
pleat
1-1/4"
folds

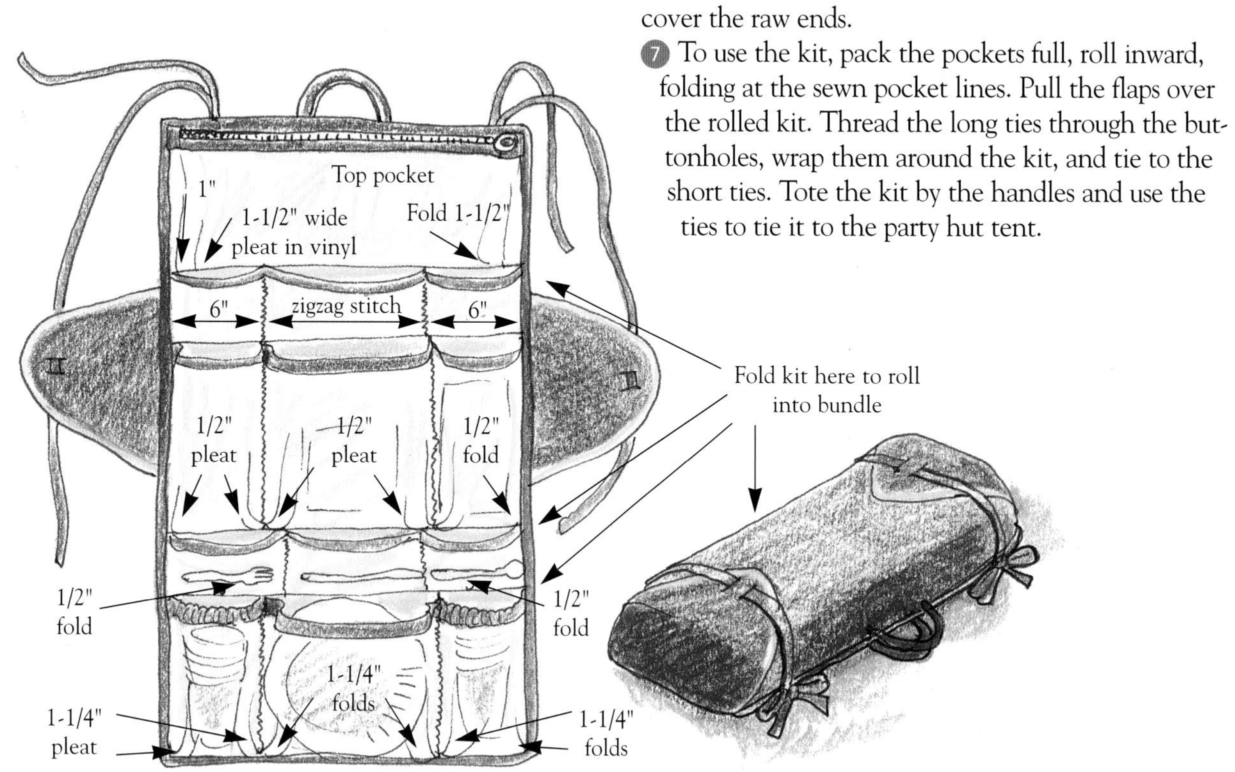

Scale 1 square = 1"

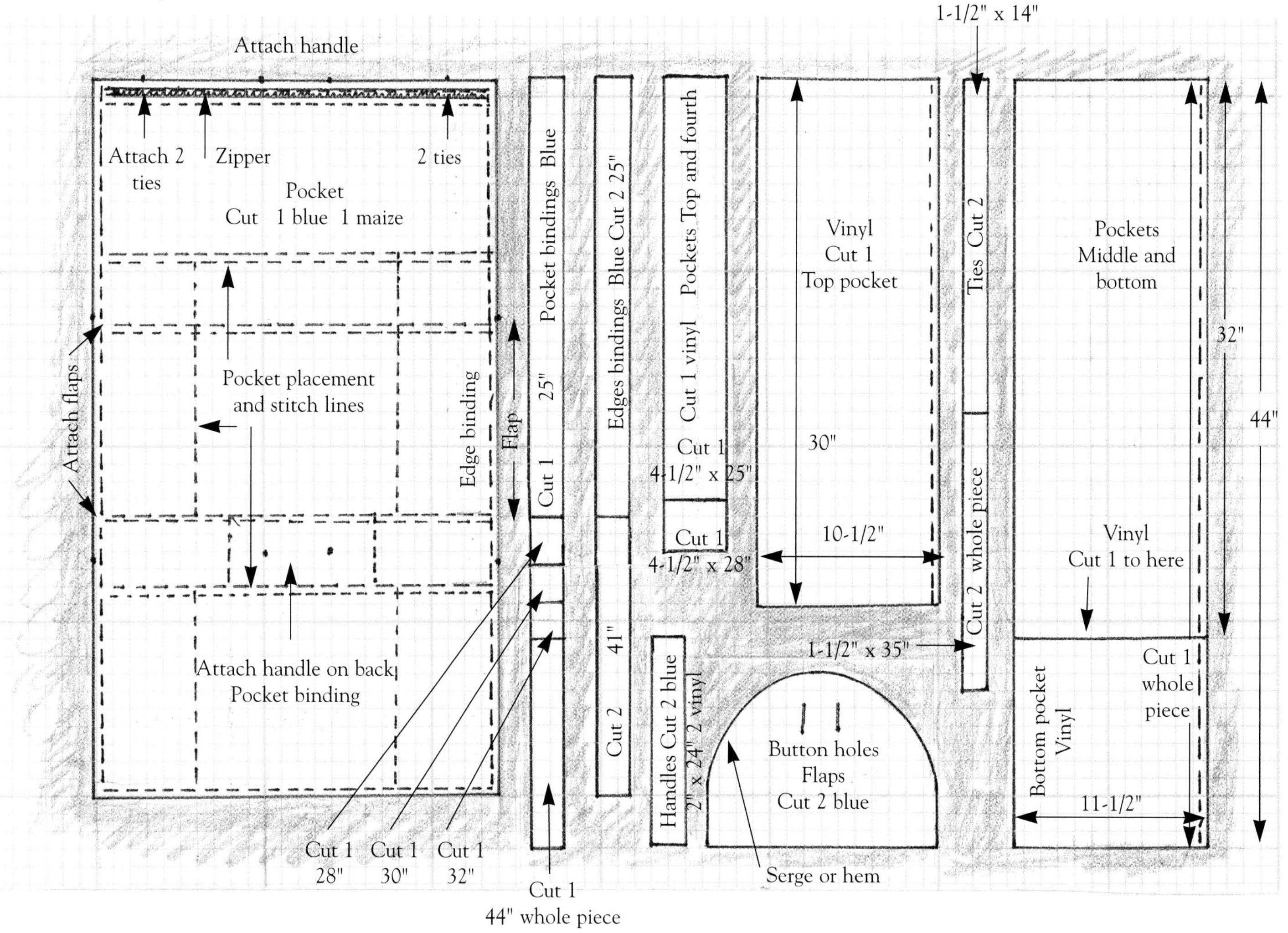

Attach handle
Attach 2
ties
Zipper
2 ties
Pocket
Cut 1 blue 1 maize
Attach flaps
Pocket placement
and stitch lines
Edge binding
Attach handle on back
Pocket binding
Cut 1
28"
Cut 1
30"
Cut 1
32"
Pocket bindings Blue
25"
Cut 1
Flap
Cut 1
44" whole piece
Edges bindings Blue Cut 2 25"
41"
Cut 2
Pockets Top and fourth
Cut 1 vinyl
Cut 1
4-1/2" x 25"
Cut 1
4-1/2" x 28"
Handles Cut 2 blue
2" x 24" 2 vinyl
Vinyl
Cut 1
Top pocket
30"
10-1/2"
1-1/2" x 35"
Button holes
Flaps
Cut 2 blue
Serge or hem
1-1/2" x 14"
Ties Cut 2
Cut 2 whole piece
Pockets
Middle and
bottom
32"
44"
Vinyl
Cut 1 to here
Cut 1
whole
piece
Bottom pocket
Vinyl
11-1/2"

Chapter 10

Sewing for Your Lanai

Photographed at Don and Audrey Busse's Lanai and Caged Pool

Tropical Florida appears wonderfully exotic to my Michigan eyes. Mop-topped palm trees nod hello at the airport. Gulf of Mexico waves bring beautiful shells to the sandy beaches. Remarkable fish swim the warm waters. Pelicans and Great Blue Herons come to the back door hoping for a handout. No wonder I chose Florida flora and fauna for a theme for the following group of projects. There's no sewing on two of these projects, just gluing and painting.

Audrey and Don Busse's caged pool has Florida-themed projects: a local shell-motif canvas table-top, Gulf of Mexico fish floorcloth, spiral shell pillows, and a wavy plant cover. The wall hanging by Leslie Masters features iron-on adhesive no-sew quilting. Photo by Jane Letchworth.

Project 36:

Canvas-covered table

These pre-owned tables from the Sarasota Woman's Exchange had fake wood Formica tops and black bases, but good basic lines. Also in my stash of things-too-good-to-throw-away was some unsized artist's canvas. Gluing on the artist's canvas avoids any possibility of chipped paint over the Formica. Florida shells provided a motif to paint with artist's acrylic paints on the bottom table. Its polyurethane coating has lasted well on the lanai. Here's how to make your own.

ABOVE: The diamond pattern painted on this canvas-covered kitchen table echoes a nearby china cabinet. The painted words say "What's for lunch? What's for lunch?"

LEFT: An old table covered with artist's canvas is an ideal surface for painting. A motif of Florida shells bring the beach to the pool.

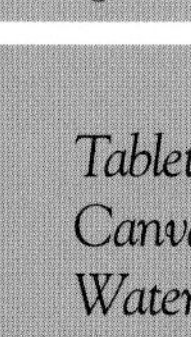

You need:

*Tableto*p
Canvas to cover with 4″ more on all sides
Water-soluble glue (Sobol, Tacky, or Elmer's)
Undercoat paint
Artist's acrylic paint (finer ground and richer colors than house paint)
Polyurethane
Tools: sponge, scraper, scissors, brayer (roller), utility knife, paint brush, artist's paint brushes, water jar, plastic drop cloth, wax-based colored pencils that won't bleed into water paint

FABRICS: Artist's canvas comes in various weights and widths up to 6', but you only need to overlap your table edges by 4″. Buy unsized canvas to stretch and mold to your project from art supply or fabric stores. Gesso makes the canvas ready for painting. Use artist's acrylic paint, oil paint, or collage to create images on it.

Making the table:

Note: For any paint project work outside or in a well-ventilated space.

❶ Base: Refinish the table base first. For the antique look shown (opposite page, bottom left), put a light-weight plastic bag over your hand and spray blue-green lacquer on your bag-covered palm. Wad your hand, then pat the wet paint on the legs to print a wrinkled paint pattern.

❷ Top:

A. Glue the canvas on the tabletop:

Cut the canvas 4″ larger than the tabletop on all sides.

① Cut the canvas to cover the top and sides with 4″ to spare on all sides.

② Dampen the canvas top and squeeze out extra water.

Spread the dampened canvas on the glue-covered table.

③ Squirt glue over the entire top then use the scraper to smooth it. Wash glue off the scraper.

④ Spread the damp canvas on the top and smooth it. Roll the top with the brayer to press the canvas into the glue and eliminate all air bubbles. Smooth and stretch the canvas toward the edges with your hands. It does get gooey as the glue comes through. Pull the canvas at the edges to make the surface smooth and taut. This stretching is necessary to get a smooth top.

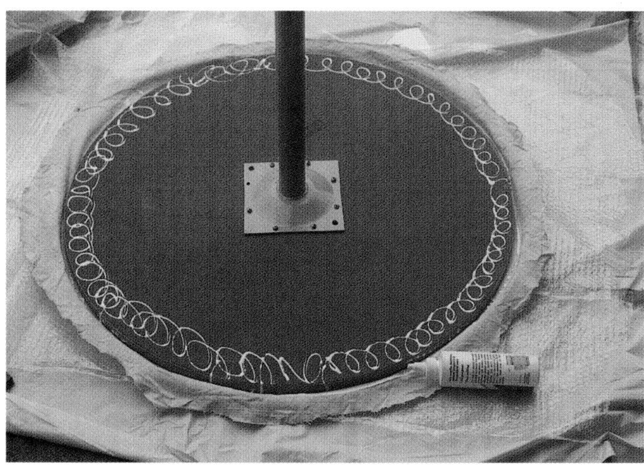

Turn the table over, glue the edges, and pull the canvas up until all wrinkles disappear.

⑤ Glue the edges. Flip the table over onto the drop cloth and glue around the table edge and underside, inward for 3″. Pull the canvas upward over the edge and onto the table bottom side. Keep pulling the canvas until no wrinkles remain around the edge. Canvas is flexible enough to do this.

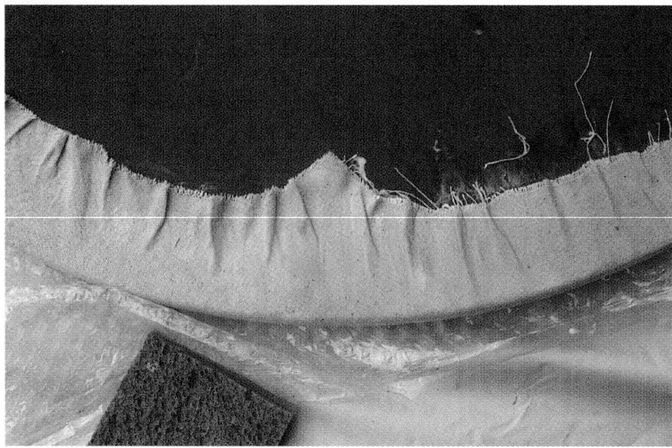

Glue the underside for 3", then stretch and pull all wrinkles to the center.

Tape the edges in place and wait until the glue is nearly dry.

⑥ Stretch the canvas on the glued underside and press the wrinkles toward the center. You won't be able to smooth all wrinkles yet because wet glue won't hold well enough. Stick duct tape over the damp edges and wait until the glue is tacky.

⑦ When the glue is tacky (2 hours?) peel off the duct tape toward the table center. Use the scraper and your fingers to stretch and push wrinkles in from the edge. Try to smooth all wrinkles 2″ in from the edge.

⑧ When the glue is nearly dry, trim away canvas on the table underside with a sharp utility knife, in 2″ from the table edge. Turn the table right-side-up to dry.

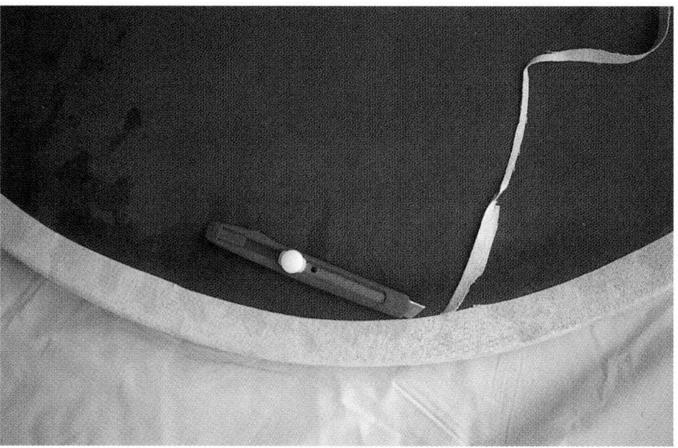

Use a sharp utility knife to trim the canvas on the underside, 2" from the edge.

B. Paint the tabletop with undercoat or gesso (a mixture of plaster and glue) for painting.

C. Paint your design with artist's acrylics. Apply the background color first. Sketch the images on with wax-based colored pencils so the lines won't run into the paint. Paint the images and let them dry.

Coat the canvas with gesso, paint on your designs with artist's acrylics, and cover with polyurethane.

D. Paint on several coats of water soluble matte-finish polyurethane. Let dry between coats.

Project 37:

Shell pillows

Beautiful beach shells are actually homes for sea creatures. The inflexible shell must grow larger as the occupant expands. The shell's growth in a spiral fashion, adding ever larger rings, made me wonder, "What if a shell-shaped pillow were made essentially the same way?" This pattern does that.

FABRICS: Glazed poly-cotton chintz comes in many colors and has the easy flexibility of tightly-woven fabric. Try other fabrics, like velvet, metallic lamé, brocade, or even felt or leather.
One pillow is stuffed with my over-supply of plastic grocery bags which do not absorb moisture in damp air. The other has fiberfill.

PATTERN: Both long and short shells: Cut one strip 3-1/2″ x 44″ and one strip tapering from 3-1/2″ to 1-1/2″ x 44″. Do not cut out the rounded end of the pillow until the shell's sides are assembled.

One glazed chintz shell pillow has fiberfill stuffing, while the other is filled with lots of plastic grocery bags.

You need:

Long shell
1 strip of rust-colored fabric. 7″ x 44″
1 piece of peach-colored fabric. 5″ x 6″
Orange/silver cord. 3 yards
Stuffing

Short shell
1 strip of peach-colored fabric. 7″ x 44″
1 piece of rust-colored fabric. 8″ x 8″
Orange/silver cord. 7′
Stuffing

Tools: fabric glue, quilting pins, scissors

Sewing the pillows:

❶ Join the wider strip to the tapering strip to make one long strip.

❷ Gather one edge of the strip using the differential feed on the serger, using a gathering foot on your sewing machine, or hand sew basting stitches. The long pillow is gathered less than the short (the long from 88″ to 77″, the short from 88″ to 66″).

Spiraled shell-shaped pillows result from sewing the gathered edge of a fabric strip to its straight edge.

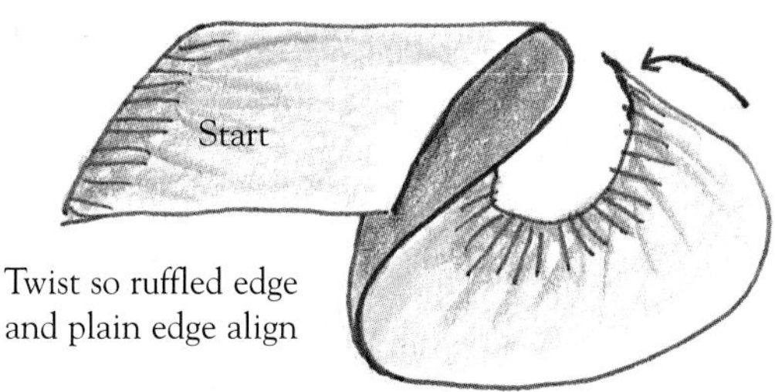

❸ At the strip's narrow end, twist once to loop the gathered edge and the ungathered edge face-to-face. Align these edges under the sewing machine foot and sew toward the length of the strip. The gathered edge on top makes a right twist shell, on the bottom a left twist. Sew these edges spiraling all the way to the top.

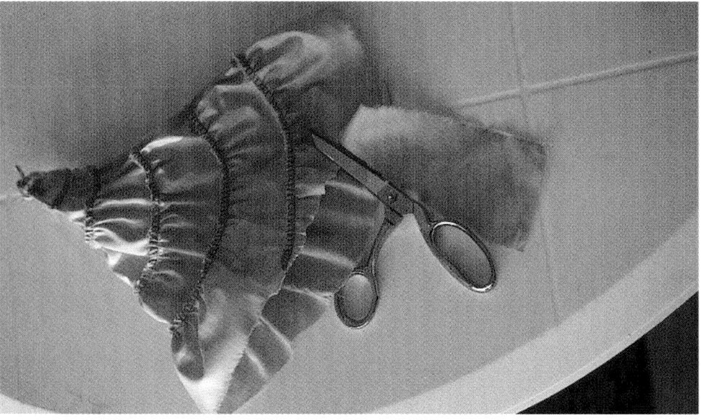

Trim off the strip's extra fabric, tapering it to the seam line (Step 5).

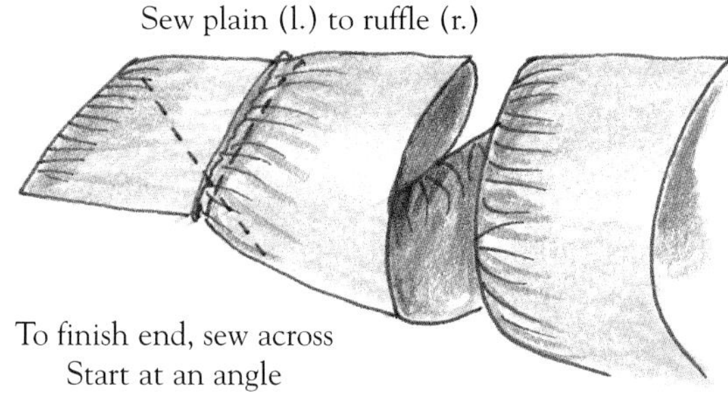

❹ Fold the shell tip and sew at an angle across the end to eliminate raw edges. Trim.

❺ At the top, trim the strip to taper a smooth edge.

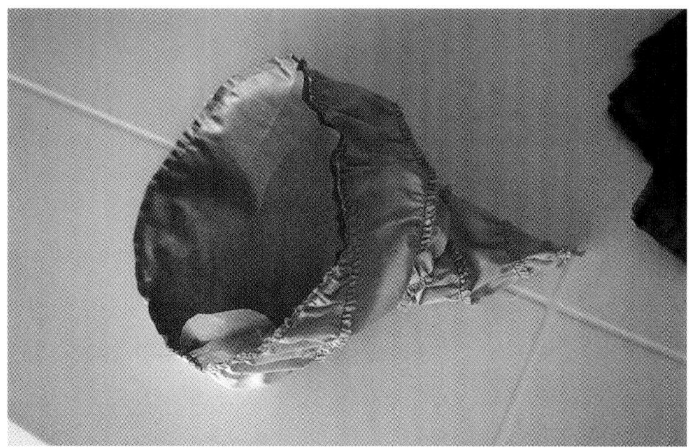

Fit the end piece to the gathered opening of the shell pillow.

❻ Gather the top edge of the shell.

❼ Trace the gathered opening size on the end fabric, add a 1/4″ seam allowance, and cut out. Pin the end to the opening face-to-face and sew, leaving a 3″ opening to turn.

Stuff the shell bit-by-bit to sculpture its shape, then sew the end closed and glue on cord trim.

❽ Turn and stuff the shell bit by bit, pushing the stuffing carefully in place to build the shape of the shell. Sew the opening closed with hidden hand stitching.

❾ Glue or sew the cord to the shell's seam.

Project 38:

Fish floorcloth

Here's another project to glue and paint fabric instead of sew. Because a fish can't pose as a shell can, use photographs or a guidebook on fish. You can paint other imagery on a floorcloth from realistic to stylized to abstract. Keep in mind the scene will be viewed from above, not as most paintings are like windows on the world. Floorcloths give an opportunity for cheerful colors and scenes in your outdoor decor. Use a pad under it to delay scratching. Several coats of polyurethane make the surface tougher than you might think. To clean, scrub with soap and water.

Artist's canvas makes a sturdy floorcloth and adds a Florida fish scene underfoot.

You need:

Artist's sized canvas. 44″ x 54″
Sobol glue
Acrylic house paint (for undercoat)
Acrylic artist paint
Source for imagery
Polyacrylic varnish
Tools: water jar, pan, Prismacolor wax pencil, wide and fine artist's paint brushes, paper towels, news papers, or other floor protector

FABRICS: Pre-sized canvas that has a surface prepared for finish painting is recommended for this project. Artist's sized canvas has a mix of glue and plaster called gesso painted on and absorbed into the fabric to make a hard, smooth ground for paint. I recommend buying sized canvas, because it is hard to size your own and keep it flat.

Making the floorcloth:

1. Roll out the canvas, sized side down. Paint the entire back of the canvas with gesso or acrylic house paint. Painting the canvas will cause it to shrink a bit. Let dry and flip over.
2. To paint the design, plan to leave 1-1/4″ border to fold under.

A. Spread canvas out on the floor or table, or staple it to the wall. Using artist's acrylics, squeeze an inch or two of yellow, green, cobalt blue, white, lavender, and sienna on the pan. Use a wide brush to mix a yellow-green color (green, white, and a touch of sienna), dilute slightly with water, and paint the top 10″. Mix blue and green and paint the next swath. Mix blue and touches of white and purple to shade downward. Paint rapidly so you can grade the colors into one another.

B. Draw the fish shapes on paper, cut out, and place and trace them on the background with a wax pencil. Paint a portrait of each fish. Add brush streaks of white and light purple across the scene for a watery look.

C. Paint a border to frame the scene. Let the paint dry completely for a day or more. Humidity affects drying.

3. Fold a 1-1/4″ hem around the edges. Clip across the corner at a 45° angle to miter the corners. Glue with Sobol or Elmer's, not a glue gun. Put a weight on top to hold. **Don't try sewing this on your machine.**
4. Varnish both the front and back of the floorcloth. Wait several days between coats so the coating won't stay sticky and attract dirt. Paint on several coats for best wear. Polyacrylic by Minwax is one of the best clear coatings. It stays the clearest and doesn't yellow.

ABOVE: Use a guidebook for authentic fish, cut out the shapes for placement, and paint them on. Use several coats of Polyacrylic by Minwax to finish.

LEFT: With a wide brush paint a watery-looking background with colors blended from yellow-green, through blue to purple.

Project 39:

Plant cover

Here's a way to dress up an ordinary plant pot or make a cracker basket for the lanai. You can coordinate this to your decor.

A large doubled circle of fabric, when gathered a few inches from the edge, causes the rope-welted edge to undulate in loops.

You need:

Green and white plaid chintz. 21″ x 21″
Blue poly-cotton broadcloth. 21″ x 26″
Rope or welting cord. 66″

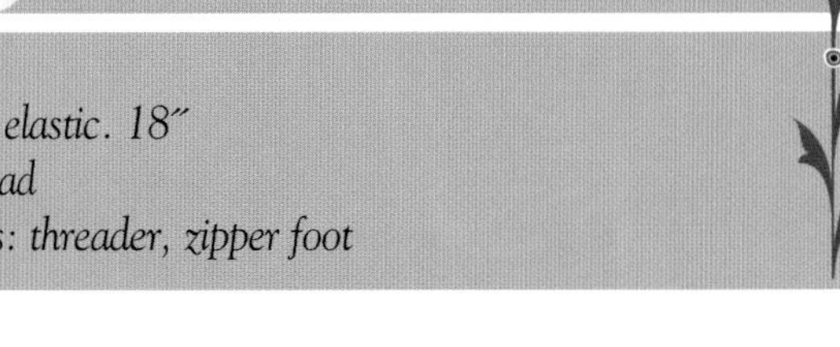

3/8″ elastic. 18″
Thread
Tools: threader, zipper foot

Measure both sides and the bottom width of your plant pot to create this cheerful cover.

PATTERN: For a 6″ tall pot, draw a 21″ circle. Fold the circle in half and trace, adding 1/2″ seam allowances to the fold. For other sizes, measure the pot sides and bottom plus 5″. Experiment with your fabric because it flexes and stretches.

Cut out one plaid 21″ circle and two blue half circles.

Sewing the cover:

1 Align the blue half circles, stitch across, leaving a 3″ center opening to turn.

2 Match the circles face-to-face and sew around them with a 1/2″ seam allowance. Turn right-side-out.

3 Measure 2″ from the edge and chalk-mark a seam line for the elastic casing,

4 Insert the rope and fit it firmly at the edge seam. Topstitch close to the rope all around using the zipper foot. This seam may be a tussle, but hang in there!

5 Topstitch the marked casing seam. Sew another line 1/2″ down, leaving a 1/2″ opening to insert the elastic. Thread the elastic, pull to the desired length, and topstitch to hold the ends. Hand sew the opening closed.

Project 40:

Diamond banner

My painter friend Leslie Masters made this handsome piece. She was inspired by the British quilting colorist Kaffe Fassett's book *Glorious Patchwork*. No sewing! All of the pieces adhere with iron-on adhesive. Leslie teaches color and design in painting, so she managed the color progressions of this piece masterfully.

Choose colorful quilting fabrics with groups of motifs; the little all-over prints don't work quite as well. See-through templates allow for centering fabric print motifs where you want them on the diamond.

Choose eighteen different print fabrics that relate and progress through changes of hue and value for the ten rows of diamonds adhered to the background fabric.

You need:

Bleached cotton muslin (for backing). 2 yards x 44″
18 selections of cotton print fabrics. From 4″ to 7″ wide x 44″ inches, depending on pattern
HeatnBond fusible backing paper. 9 yards (the non-sew type, 18″ wide)
1/2″ dowel rod. 45″
Tools: iron, rotary cutter or sharp scissors, metal ruler, diamond template, chalk marker

PATTERN: 36″ x 55″, ten diamonds across and eighteen rows up. Diamond pattern 3-1/2″ x 6″ (cut 180 pieces, no seam allowances), backing 44″ x 60″. Buy or make a diamond template 3-1/2″ x 6″ from plastic or mat board. Get a ready-made template from fabric or craft stores or sewing catalogues.

Making the banner:

❶ Select eighteen different fabrics in a color progression. This takes all day but it is the crux of success! Collect colors and patterns to see how they relate. For the colors shown you will need to compromise on some choices. Make sure your colors sing together. Notice that if you change one you may well need to change others for harmony. And a little selective discord isn't bad—it wakes up the piece.

❷ The diamonds must be cut exactly at the proper angle to fit together. First adhere the fusible to the diamond fabric back. For a non-directional pattern make a fabric row of ten overlapping diamonds 3-1/2″ x 44″. Cut HeatnBond to match and iron-on fabric strip back. Cut the diamonds apart but don't peel the paper backing yet. To select and center a motif such as the sunflower you will need more fabric and will waste some. Move the template around to find the image in the window, iron on a diamond fusible backing and cut this out.

❸ Lay out and iron the backing fabric cut to 44″ x 60″. If possible work on a padded surface where you can lay out the entire width of the fabric. Mark lines across the backing fabric every 6″. Peel off the paper backing and line up the diamonds across the fabric with center edge points on the line. When you are **sure** the placement is accurate, iron to fuse the diamond to the backing. Use a Teflon-faced iron-on paper to keep fusible from sticking. Trim up the sides (half diamonds remain) and along the diamond pattern across the bottom edge. Make a casing at the top. Iron a 2″ wide fusible strip on the top back side above the top diamond row. Fold at the center of the top diamond row to hem and iron to bond the casing.

Diamond
Cut 10 of each color

Make 18 rows
Cut 180 diamonds

Center large motifs in diamonds

5-1/2"

3"

3"

3-1/2"

No seam allowance

Chapter 11

Sewing for Your Picnic

Photographed on the Hall's Deck, Everyone's Grass

There's a freedom to outdoor eating that delights the soul. Outdoor picnics can be as casual as hot dogs and sitting on a blanket or as upscale as caviar, folding chairs, and frilly tablecloths. The following picnic has colors from informal denim-blue cambric to brash oranges, blues, and purples—a northern color range. Every color goes with grass green.

"Come join us," these exuberant colors shout, "and let's have an picnic." The patchwork tablecloth covers a Polar Fleece blanket spread out in the author's backyard.

Project 41:

Blanket

What's more basic than a blanket? At your picnic you can sit on it, mark your space, keep bugs off, fall asleep on it, and wrap up in it if the wind blows or the rain comes.

The clear vinyl back shows what's inside this blanket bag. Used as a cushion, the vinyl also keeps you from the foggy dew.

You need:

Polarfleece. 2-1/3' x 62″
Polyester (washable) ribbon. 1-1/2″ x 8-1/2 yards
Tools: scissors, thread, hand needle, yardstick

Fabrics: Polarfleece, a fabric woven from recycled plastic bottles, comes 62″ wide so it needs no seams to become a blanket—and it's washable. The must-be-washable-too ribbon edging is less flexible than the fleece, so sew it on with stitching that shapes it to the fleece such as zigzag machine stitching or hand stitching. Both the ribbon and the fleece have no wrong sides.

Other fabrics in this collection include cambric (white warp threads crossed by blue or other color), quilting cotton prints, clear vinyl, and a space-age insulating fabric described below.

Pattern: Measure a rectangle 62″ x 84″. Cut off the selvage and trim to correspond with the plaid design.

Sewing the blanket:

1. Align the ribbon faceup to the fleece so the ribbon edge overlaps 1/4″, pin, and topstitch. Be careful not to stretch the fleece. Pivot the ribbon at the corners.
2. Fold the ribbon onto the fleece to cover the seam allowances. At each corner, finger-press a right angle fold in the ribbon. Zigzag machine stitch or hand stitch the ribbon in place. The less flexible ribbon will wrinkle but the topstitching organizes the wrinkle pattern.

Note: Traditionally, Polarfleece blankets have a hand-sewn blanket stitching around the edges. To make this process even quicker, use woolly nylon thread in a three-thread flat hem to serge the quilt edge. Round the corners for no-stop serging and you're done!

Project 42:

Blanket bag

This bag not only stores your blanket and keeps it dry, but it also makes an easy carrying case and provides a cushion to sit on.

You need:

Medium-weight denim. 18″ x 36″
6 mil. clear vinyl plastic. 16″ square
Print fabric or other trim. 6″ square
Zipper. 24″
Blue thread
Fuchsia machine embroidery thread
Fusible. 6″ square
Tools: scissors, ruler

ABOUT FABRICS: One side of this bag is made from a twill-weave blue denim, like the chambray, woven of white warp threads and blue cross threads. The other is 6 mil. clear plastic, which is waterproof, yet sewable.

PATTERN: Bag 15″ x 15″. To make this bag, fold the blanket in half, then in quarters. Fold the long side in thirds, then in half to make a bundle about 15″ square x 4″ thick, or fold your blanket to the size cushion you want and make the bag to fit.

Measure these pieces (includes 1/2″ seam allowance): A bag side 16″ x 16″ (cut one denim and one plastic), B bag bottom 16 ″ x 5″ (cut one denim), C bag sides 12″ x 5″ (cut two denim), D bag top, cut two strips 25″ x 2-1/2″ of denim, E bag handle 2-1/2″ x 9″, F motif cut one 5″ square of patterned fabric or other design.

Sewing the bag:

1. Motif: Iron the fusible on the F motif back, trim to size, and iron onto the A center bag side. Satin-stitch to hold and delineate the design.

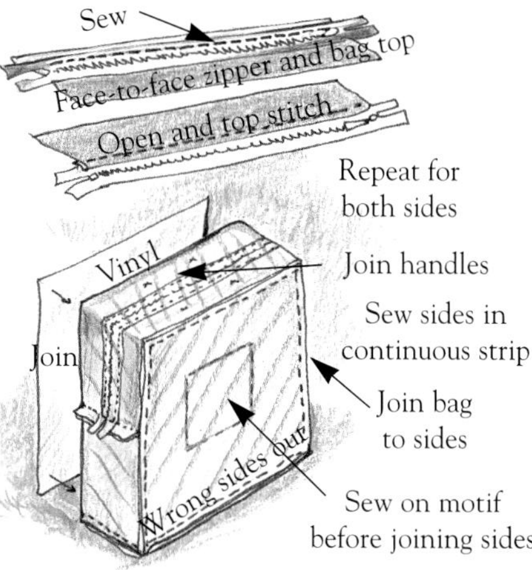

2. Fold the E handle face-to-face lengthwise, sew a 1/2″ seam allowance, turn the strip.
3. Align the zipper with the D top strips. Lay the zipper face-to-face with one strip and serge the edges. Open flat and topstitch 1/8″ from the fold. Align and repeat for the other side.
4. Join the zipper D strip ends to the C side ends face-to-face and serge or sew. Join the B bottom to the C sides face-to-face and serge. Center the handle 9-1/2″ from each side seam on the D bag top and satin-stitch to secure.
5. Align the A bag side with the assembled sides. Match the bottom corner seams with the bag corners face-to-face. Pin or hold in place. Serge or sew to join. Open the zipper. Repeat for the other side. Turn right-side-out.

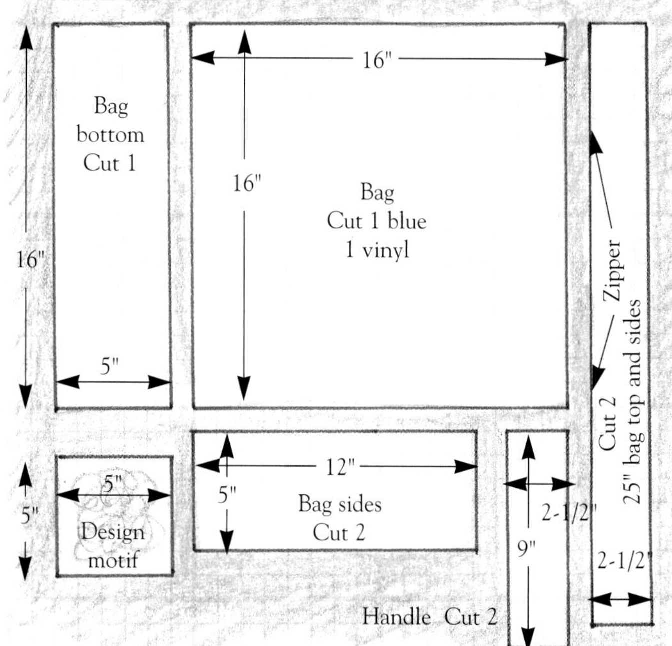

Project 43:

Lined basket

This versatile basket has gone on picnics, toted miscellaneous objects, and even carried the cat to the vet (rattan can be washed). Fitting in an insulating lining keeps things warm, dry, and clean.

Polarfleece makes up into a quick blanket hemmed with a plaid ribbon edging. Fold the blanket into the bag to carry or sit on.

Here's an old basket renewed with a removable poplin lining. The lining is filled with Thermal Fleece, a thin insulation developed by the space program.

You need:

Basket	*Matching thread*
Fabric. 2 yards x 44″	*Velcro tabs (two sets)*
Thermal Fleece or other quilting bat. 40″ x 44″	*Plastic panel or mat board. 10-1/2″ x 15-1/2″*
Elastic or cord to tie. 54″	*Tools: scissors, yardstick, pencil, bias tape device*

ABOUT FABRICS: Blue cambric fabric covers an insulation material called Thermal Fleece. An outer layer of metallic film has good heat retention coupled with a fleece layer for body. It is lightweight and easy to cut, sew, and handle, plus it is machine washable in case the cat needs another trip to the vet. Lacking this, wrap quilting-bat fiberfill with a strong plastic bag.

PATTERN: Measure your basket. Fit the cover to the basket outside. When seamed, it will fit inside.
My basket measures 11″ x 16″ x 11″ high, plus the lid.
Cut these fabric pieces: two bag linings 16″ x 38″, four ends 11″ x 11″, one cord slot 5″ x 56″, one lid 22″ x 18″, one tie 1-1/2″ x 36″ (cut in two later)
Cut these fleece: one bag lining 16″ x 38″, two ends 11″ x 11″, lid- 21″ x 18″
Cut one mat board piece 10-1/2″ x 15-1/2″

Sewing the liner:

❶ Make the basket lining:

A. Stack two bag linings, enclosing the fleece lining. Stack two end linings covering fleece for both ends.

B. Match three sides of the end stack to the bag lining stack. Serge or sew, trim, and overcast the seam allowance. Repeat for the other end. Fit this into the basket and take in seams to fit.

C. Seam across the slot. Measure elastic to fit the rim snugly and tie. Fold the slot over the elastic. Fit the slot to the liner face-to-face and sew. The slot folds down over the basket rim.

❷ Lid:

A. Hem across the 22″ side of the lid fabric. Sew Velcro tabs to the hem, 1″ from one side and 1″ in from the center fold. Sew the other tabs 4″ down from the hem on the opposite side to match.

B. Align the fabric lid to the fleece lid. Fold fabric face-to-face and seam across the unhemmed end and along the side to the hem make an envelope.

C. Make a double fold and topstitch the tie full length. Cut in two. Sew the center of one tie to the seamed end of the lid. Sew the other to the fold end of the lid (see next).

D. The lid fold: Slide the mat board or stiff liner into the removable lid envelope. Fold the flap over to align Velcro tabs.

E. Push the tie ends up through the basket lid in two places and tie to secure.

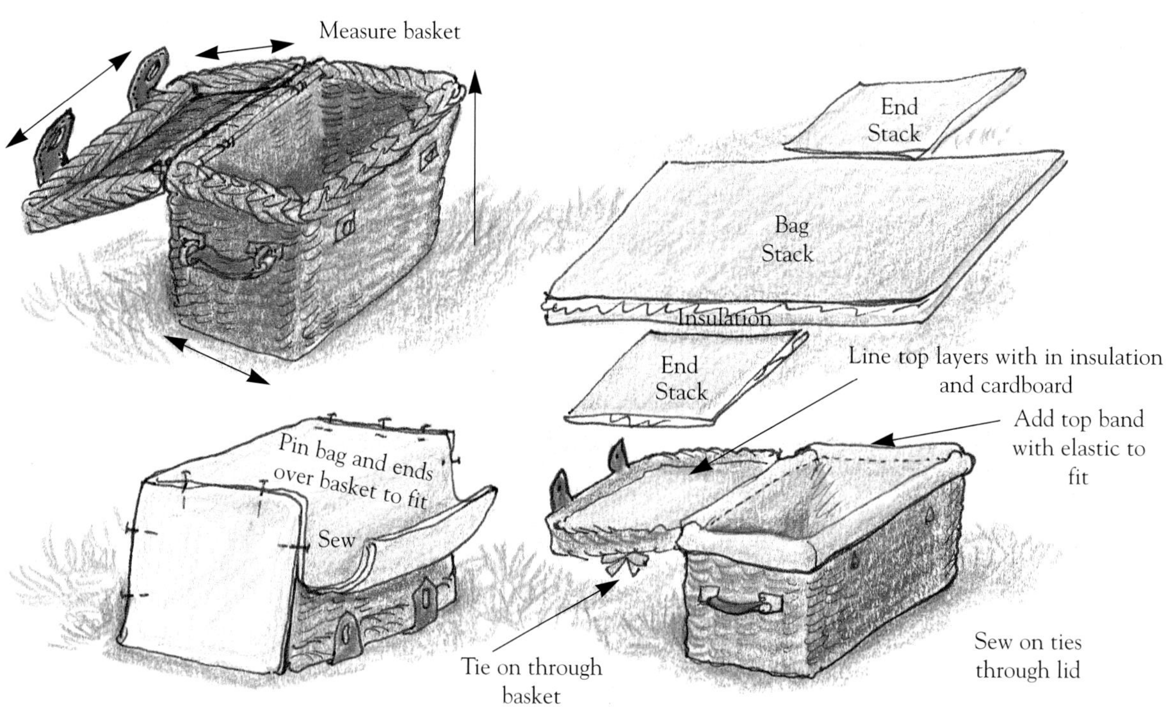

Project 44:

Place mats & napkins

Colors go from muted to zing for the mat flip-sides and napkins. The versatile poly-cotton cambric has no wrong side.

Each quilted place mat has a different free-motion sewn "sketch" next to a cutlery pocket with a napkin matching the reverse side. (Or go wild and mix the napkins!)

You need:

Blue cambric (for the mats). 1-1/3 yards x 44″
Six colors of fabric (for the mat backs and napkins). 18″ x 34″ (each)
Quilting bat or filler. 36″ x 44″
Blue serger threads
White thread
Tools: hand needle, yardstick, pencil

PATTERN: Finished mats are 13″ x 17″. Measure and cut the mat, the back, and the filler (each 14″ x 18″). Cut blue pockets 5-1/2″ x 8-1/2″. Cut pocket trim one of each color 5-1/2″ x 2″. Cut each napkin 18″ square.

Sewing:

1 The place mat:

A. Stack the mat and back face-to-face and add the filler to the stack. Sew the edges, leaving a 5″ opening to turn. Trim filler seam allowance and corners. Turn and press. Hand sew the opening closed. Repeat for all six.

B. Pocket: Fold the trim lengthwise (face out), align to the pocket top, and sew . Fold the pocket/trim down 1-1/2″ onto pocket, seam allowance upward, and topstitch along the seam line. Fold a 1/4″ hem in three sides of the pocket, press, and pin. Repeat for all.

C. Topstitch around the mat 5/8″ from the edge. Place the pocket in 1″ and up 1″ from the lower left corner, pin, and topstitch three sides. Set the machine for pattern stitching or free-motion sewing and quilt the mat.

Project 45:

Tablecloth

About quilt construction:

In quilt design, like playing with colored papers, you can add and subtract colors at will to experiment with various combinations, try wild colors, and even remove a "wrong" square later. This pieced tablecloth uses the same fabrics as the place mats, minus the taming blue, plus assorted strong, heavier colors.

The tablecloth is constructed log cabin quilting style from the center square outward. This technique allows for adjusting by making the interior borders wider or narrower as needed. The strip technique makes sewing multiple blocks quicker and easier. Sew rows of strips, then cut across the assembled strip to make rows of squares. Sew the square rows together to make the blocks and strips.

Strange colors and patterns can get along when settled down in a repeated pattern and controlled with black and white. Sections of the tablecloth are strip-quilted for easier joining of tiny squares. It is assembled log cabin-style from the center out.

You need:

Tablecloth quilt size 50″ x 50″
Fabric amounts and strips to cut:
Center Square. Cream 16″
1st border. Dark green 1-1/2″ x 18″ (four strips)
Checkerboard rows
Black 2″ x 32″ (eight strips)
White 2″ x 32″ (eight strips)
Black 3″ x 3″ (four squares)
2nd border. Maroon 2″ x 22″ (four strips)
3rd border. Gold 1-1/2″ x 23″ (four strips)
Next row
Cream 2-1/2″ x 12″ (eight strips)
Black 2-1/2″ x 2-1/2″ (four)
Patchwork blocks
Four 3″ x 36″ strips of each of these eight color prints: red, green, ocher, purple, aqua, navy/orange, fuchsia, and pea green
Black 2″ x 9″ (twelve inset strips)
Navy 2″ x 9″ (twelve corner borders)
Apple print 7″ x 7″ print (four corners)
4th border
Orange 1-1/2″ x 44″ (four strips)
Aqua 1-1/2″ squares (four)
Outside border
Maroon 5″ x 44″ (four strips)
Fuchsia 4″ squares (four)
Backing. 51″ x 51″ square cream (use sheeting or seam as necessary)

ABOUT FABRICS: An exuberant assortment of quilting-weight fabrics serves as a pallet of colors. Some are all cotton (easier to hand sew) and some a poly-cotton mix, but all are washable. These fabrics tear along the grain line for strip construction and borders. Dimensions for fabric give 1/2″ seam allowances to trim to 1/4″, allowing leeway.

PATTERN: Follow the diagram given.

Sewing the tablecloth:

1 Assemble the strip blocks:

A. For the checkerboard strip, sew black and white alternating strips together into one strip 17″ x 32″. Cut the strip in half across and sew black to white, cut twice again, and join. Flip one strip and join black to white across the row. Repeat to make four checkered strips 3″ wide and 17″ long.

B. For the patchwork blocks, sew four strips of colors as shown (A). Repeat. Sew the second set of colors (B). Repeat. Join and sew sets A and B together. Repeat. This makes two strips of each set of four colors 36″ long. Cut the strips crosswise into twelve 3″ wide strips of four colors. Join the set A to B to A to B to make twelve blocks of sixteen squares (8″ square plus seam allowances).

C. For corner patchwork blocks sew navy strips to opposite sides of the print square. Trim off the extra. Join navy strips to each remaining side. Make four blocks.

2 Assemble the tablecloth:

Center and Row 2. Sew a dark green strip to one cream edge and trim off extra. Turn and repeat for all four edges.

Row 3. Pin and sew one checkered strip to one green strip. Sew a checkered strip to the opposite green strip. Join two black squares to the ends of the remaining checkered strips. Sew each to a green strip.

Row 4. Sew or serge a maroon strip to one checkered strip edge and trim off extra. Turn and repeat for all four edges.

Row 5. Sew or serge a gold strip to one maroon edge and trim off extra. Turn and repeat for all four edges.

Row 6. Join a 1-1/2″ black center strip to the cream strip. Repeat four times. Sew the black strip to the second cream strip. Repeat four times. Join and sew one strip to the gold strip. Repeat for the opposite gold strip. Sew two black corners to both ends of two cream strips. Join each to a remaining gold strip.

Row 7. Join these: a patchwork block/black strip/block/strip/block. Repeat four times.

Join a block row to the cream strip. Repeat on the opposite side. Join two corner blocks at each end of a block row. Repeat. Join these rows to the remaining cream strips.

Row 8. Join an orange strip to the block row. Repeat on the opposite side. Sew two aqua corner squares to each end of two orange strips. Sew these to the remaining block rows.

Row 9. Join a maroon strip to the orange row. Repeat on the opposite side. Sew two fuchsia corner squares to each end of two maroon strips. Sew these to the remaining orange strips.

❸ Finish the tablecloth:

A. Align the piece top with the same size backing. Sew around the edge leaving an 8″ opening to turn. Clip off the seam allowance corners. Turn and sew the opening closed.

B. Pin the layers together and hand or machine quilt in the ditch.

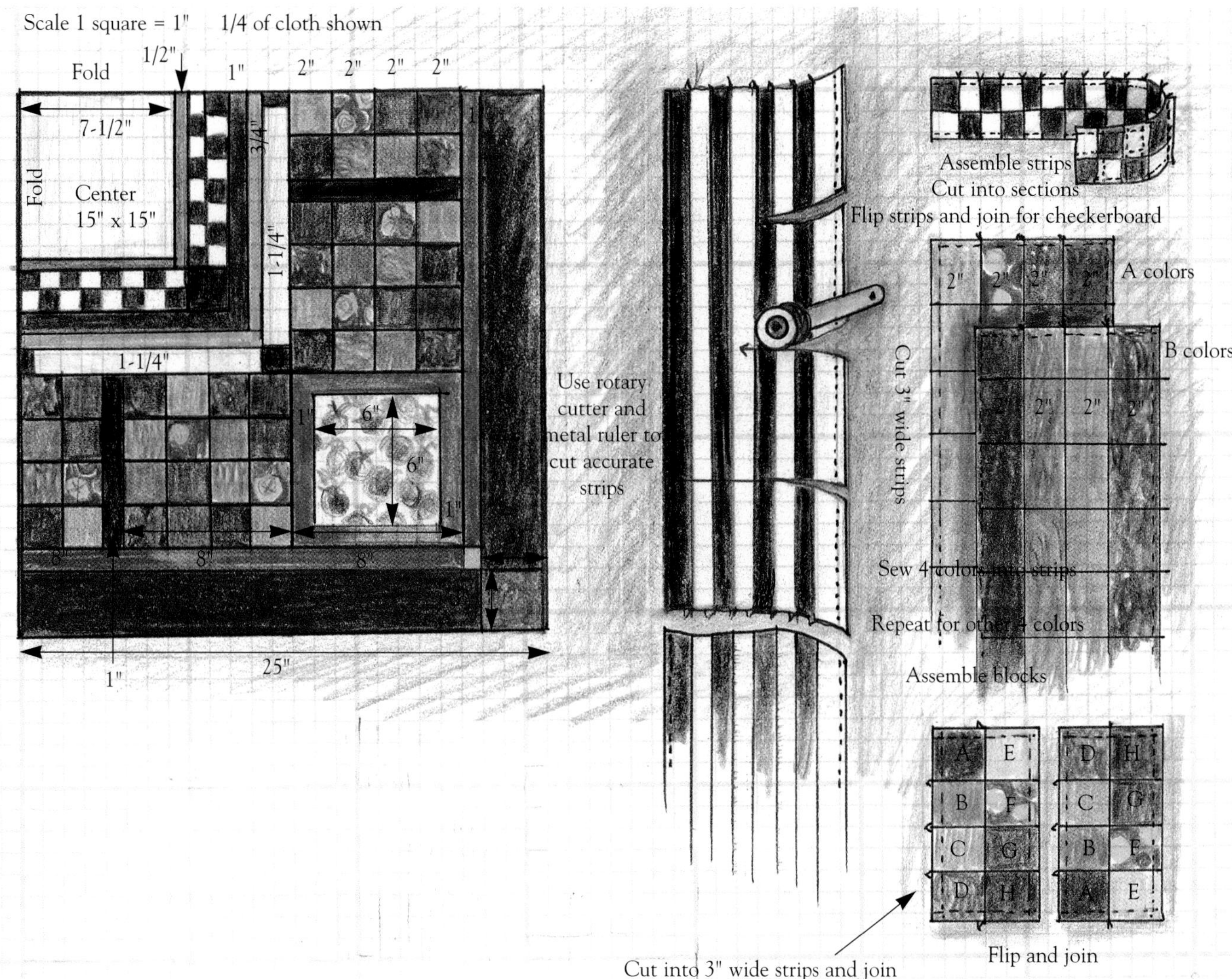

Chapter 12

Sewing for Your Spa

Photographed at Wallace and Jane Letchworth's Tea House

Wallace and Jane Letchworth have created an oriental-flavored enclave on the bay. Every detail from oriental antiques to contemporary paintings is beautifully displayed. Glimpses of their front yard and tea house spa by the bay appear in these photographs taken by Jane, a professional photographer.

The serene elegance of Wallace and Jane Letchworth's teahouse with spa on Little Sarasota Bay inspired the design of this collection. Photo by Jane Letchworth.

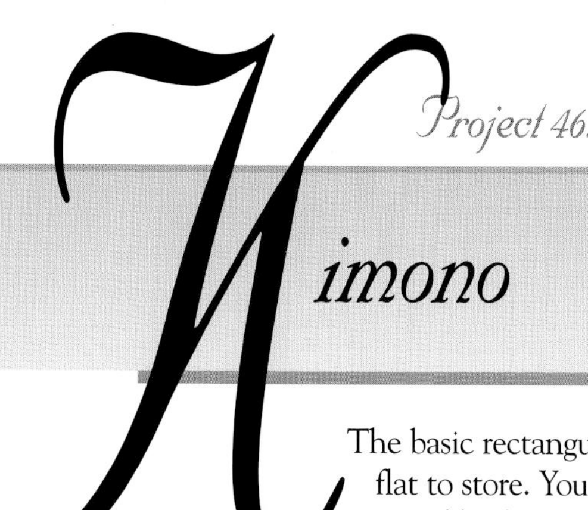

Project 46:

Kimono

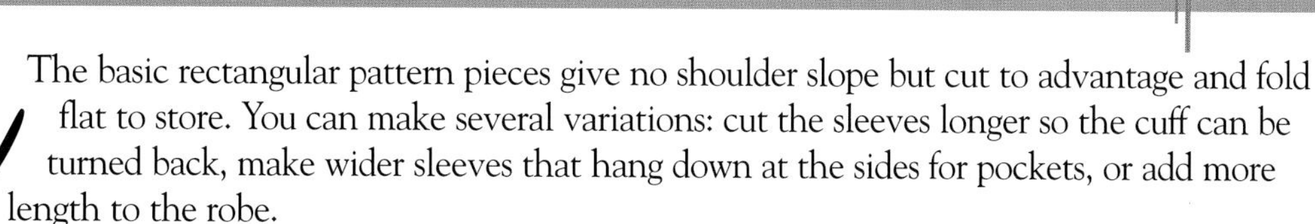

The basic rectangular pattern pieces give no shoulder slope but cut to advantage and fold flat to store. You can make several variations: cut the sleeves longer so the cuff can be turned back, make wider sleeves that hang down at the sides for pockets, or add more length to the robe.

Pat Hall and daughter Briana wear kimonos made from the same pattern, but different fabrics—and Briana helped make hers.

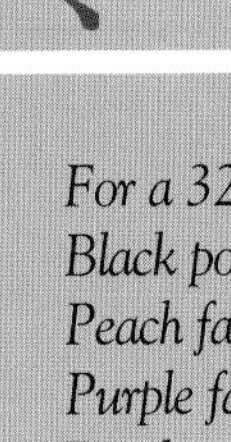

You need:

For a 32″ robe
Black polyester fabric. 2-1/3 yards x 44″
Peach fabric (for cuffs). 6″ x 44″
Purple fabric (for neck band). 18″ x 44″
Peach, purple, black, khaki, silver, gold/black and two gold metallic strips. 2″ x 44″ (one each color)
Metallic gold fabric (for back stripe). 6″ x 33″
Tools: rotary cutter, yardstick or metal ruler, wax pencil, scissors, pins

ABOUT FABRICS: Best are lightweight polyester or silk fabrics to give the characteristic drape of a traditional kimono. Make this in terry cloth for a bulkier look, or cotton for washability. Be sure your metallic fabrics are strong because some woven metallic threads fray on serged seams.

PATTERN: This medium size fits most people. For a larger size, add more width to pieces A and B, and lengthen sleeves C. Draw the pattern from the diagram directly on fabric and cut out. The sleeves, back, cuffs, band, and tie are all rectangles. Front sides 13″ x 33″, from 12″ up the inner edge taper straight to 10″ at the top.

Trim:

Piece the trim strips.

1 Cut eight strips 2″ x 44″ (the width of fabric) of peach, purple, black, khaki, silver, gold/black, and two gold.

2 Sew or serge the strips together lengthwise to 44″ x 14″. Cut across in half, match,and sew two pieces together. Repeat four times. Press on the wrong side to align seam allowances one way and serge or overcast the strip's edges.

3 Align a patched strip on each tapered front piece and baste the edges. Measure the strip 1-1/2″ wide, fold a hem, and topstitch. Repeat for the sleeves, measuring the strip in 2-1/2″ from the edge.

4 Cut the back in two halves. Align the back strip to the edges, sew, fold seam allowances onto the black, and topstitch.

Assembly:

1 Match the fronts with the back at the shoulder, tapered edges to the center, outside corners matched, and serge.

2 Fold the sleeve and pin the fold to the shoulder seam. Align the sleeve and body edges and serge. Repeat.

3 Match the robe and sleeve side seams and serge. Repeat.

4 Fold the cuff widthwise face-to-face and seam. Turn, press, fold the cuff lengthwise right-sides-out, and press the fold. Match the cuff to the sleeve face-to-face and serge. Topstitch the seam allowance to flat fell this seam.

5 Serge the robe's bottom edge, fold a 1″ hem, and topstitch or blind hem in place.

6 Match the neck band to the robe. Unpin the ends, fold the band face-to-face, and sew across the end at the robe hem. Trim and turn. Repin the band, serge to join, and topstitch the seam allowance onto the black fabric.

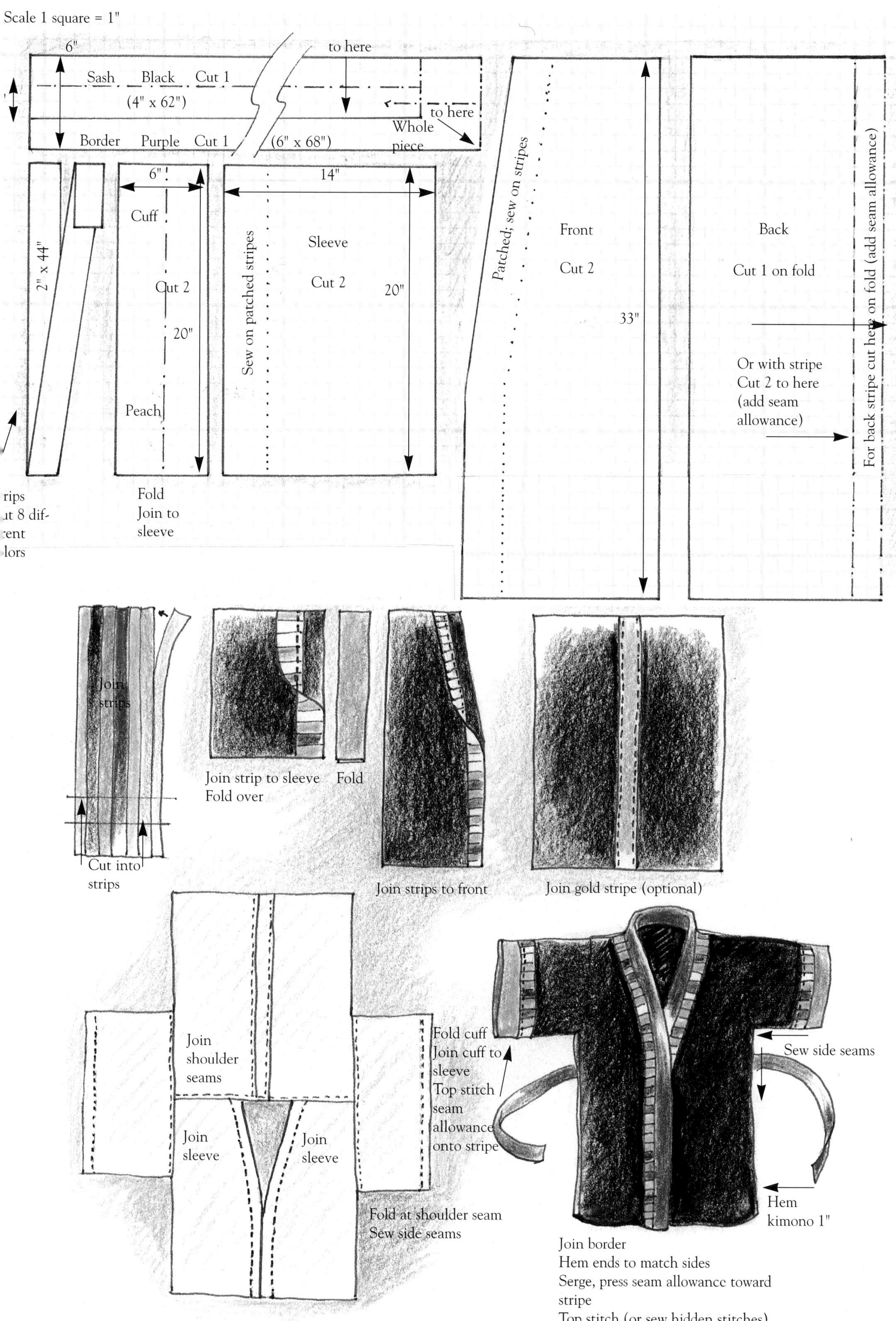

Scale 1 square = 1"
6"
Sash Black Cut 1
(4" x 62")
to here
to here
Whole piece
Border Purple Cut 1
(6" x 68")
2" x 44"
rips
ut 8 dif-
rent
lors
6"
Cuff
Cut 2
20"
Peach
Fold
Join to
sleeve
14"
Sew on patched stripes
Sleeve
Cut 2
20"
Patched; sew on stripes
Front
Cut 2
33"
Back
Cut 1 on fold
Or with stripe
Cut 2 to here
(add seam
allowance)
For back stripe cut here on fold (add seam allowance)
Join
strips
Cut into
strips
Join strip to sleeve
Fold over
Fold
Join strips to front
Join gold stripe (optional)
Join
shoulder
seams
Join
sleeve
Join
sleeve
Fold cuff
Join cuff to
sleeve
Top stitch
seam
allowance
onto stripe
Fold at shoulder seam
Sew side seams
Sew side seams
Hem
kimono 1"
Join border
Hem ends to match sides
Serge, press seam allowance toward
stripe
Top stitch (or sew hidden stitches)

Project 47:

Pillow

These pillows are oriental in flavor. How? The pictorial design element, the subtle colors, and the contrast of both rich satins and natural linen. Yet they are American in design. How? The larger scale, random machine embroidery, and imagery in photo-transfer technique. These, like so much contemporary art, are an international mix of styles and ideas.

Enjoy your favorite scenes by photo-transferring them onto fabric, then add rich fabrics as in these pillows showing a coi pond and Enchantment lilies in bloom.

You need:

Regular bed pillow. 18″ x 24″
Tight-weave poly-cotton white fabric (for image). 12″ x 10″
Peach polyester satin (for frame). 12″ x 14″
Black poly-cotton (for welting). 4″ x 20″
Canvas (for inner backing). 12″ x 18″
Taupe tapestry weave (for inserts). 5″ x 18″
Dark natural linen (for sides). 12″ x 18″
Silver/gold/white brocade (for back). 27″ x 20″
Taupe rope (for welting). 72″ (plus)
Velcro or zipper. 18″
Gold machine embroidery thread
Regular sewing thread
Cording welt. 36″
Fiberfill stuffing
Tools: 36″ metal ruler

PHOTO TRANSFER: Select a photograph that suits your idea. These came from two favorite gardens: my own when the lilies bloom and a Florida artist's lily pond under a huge banyan tree where frisky coi swim. Have your image photocopied onto transfer paper (like Photo-Trans R SC, Xerox). The reversed image is placed face-down on fabric then heat- and pressure-applied to transfer the emulsion. Print and photo shops will transfer for you or kits are available to make your own. (See Sources)

ABOUT FABRICS: Select smooth, tightly-woven white or light fabric for true colors on photos. Or get some unusual effects by transferring onto various colored fabrics. I'm all for experimenting. Here a photo on chintz is complimented by the tan fabric natural linen and the peach and purple polyester satin in a heavy-weight.

PATTERN: Enlarge your image to 10″ x 8″ or redesign the pillow top to fit your design. Measure these pieces. Center strip: photo 10″ x 8″, frame two pieces 10″ x 5″ peach, backing 10″ x 18″ canvas, welting two pieces 4″ x 18″ black, inserts two 1-1/2″ x 18″ ecru mattelesse, sides two 5-1/2″ x 18″ linen, backing- two 13″ x 18″ brocade. NOTE: Add 1″ seam allowance to allow for quilting and transferring.

Transferring the photo image:

1. Lay the reversed photo printed on transfer paper face down on smooth fabric with a 1″ seam allowance (trim to size later).
2. Angle pins through each photo corner into the ironing board cover.
3. Press with the hottest setting for 3 to 5 minutes. Press, not iron, the entire image, applying pressure.
4. Pull up the backing corner to test. If it sticks, peel the backing. If not, press more, then peel.

Sewing the pillow:

1. Square the photo fabric with 1/2″ seam allowance lines pencil-drawn on the back.

A. Align frame top and bottom pieces to the image face-to-face, sew, open, and press.

B. Stack the inner backing, fiberfill, and image and pin together.

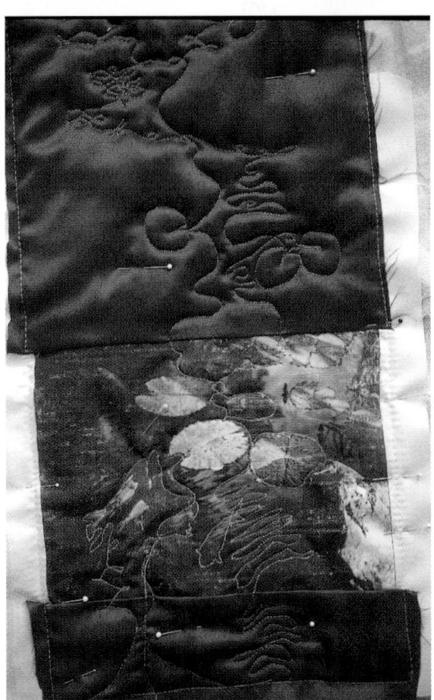

ABOVE: Stack the transferred photo and surrounding fabrics on fiberfill and backing to quilt the layers together. (That's my old Singer Genie portable sewing machine.)

RIGHT: Outline various random details of the transferred photo and continue free-motion quilting similar images on the added fabrics.

C. Quilt the center strip by free-motion stitching around various elements in the photo and continue onto the satin frame. Quilting may pull the fabric. Draw new seam lines on the inner backing.

D. Align the folded welting with the center strip face-to-face overlapping the seam line 3/8˝ toward the center. Baste.

E. Join the inset to the side. Repeat. Join these to the center strip.

2 Back: Align a pair of Velcro strips, each piece along one side of the back center edges, pin, and sew.

3 Assembly: On the top and back measure 3˝ from each corner, fold a tuck, and baste the seam line. Align the welting (rope inward) with the pillow top edges, pin, and baste. Match the pillow back to the pillow top and sew. Open the Velcro to turn and insert the pillow.

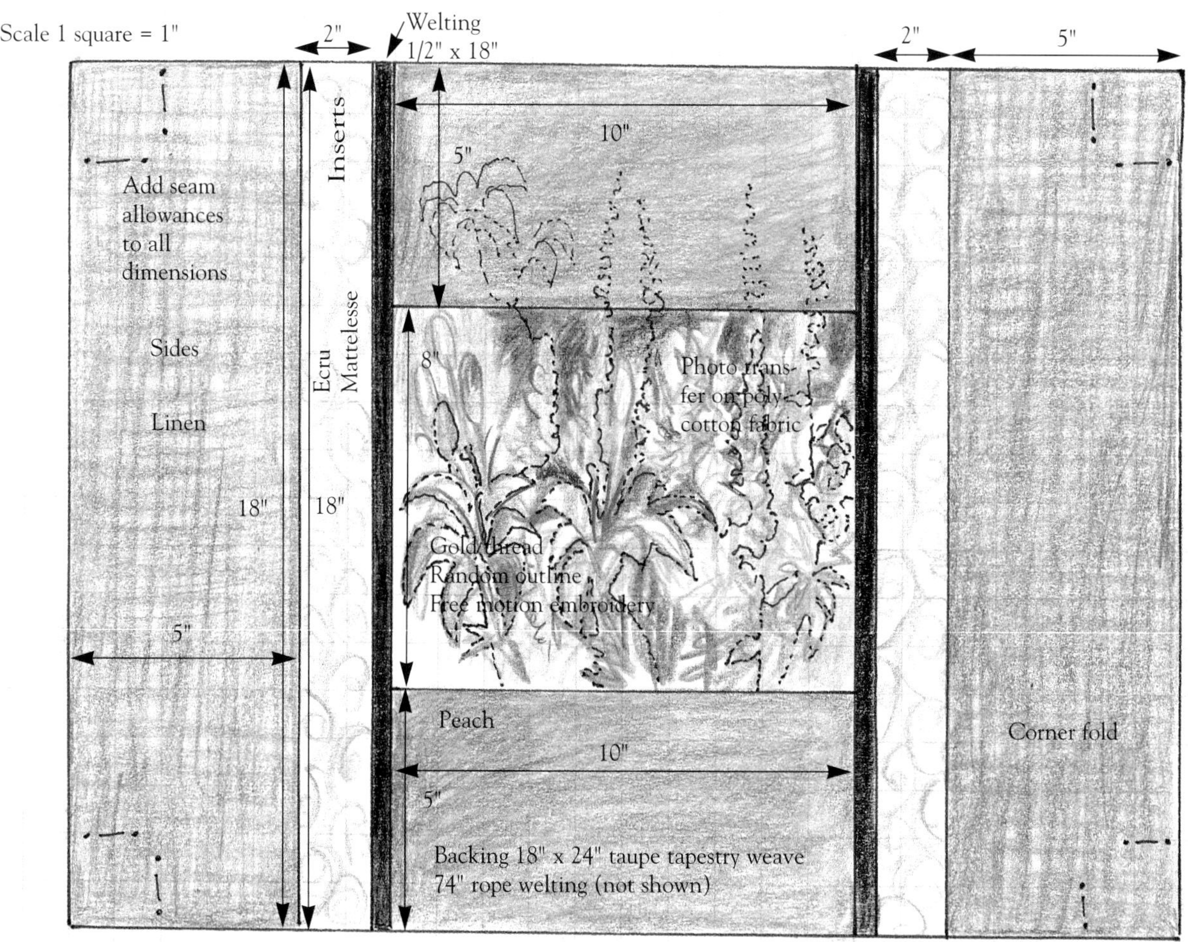

Project 48:

Bolster pillow

This pillow is made the same as the one above except for the shape. Use the fabric dimensions below and instructions above as indicated.

You need:

1 bag Polyfiberfill
Tight-weave fabric in white or eggshell (for image). 9″ x 12″
Peach polyester satin (for frame). 3″ x 12″
Purple polyester satin (for frame). 4″ x 12″
Purple polyester satin (for frame). 16″ x 12″
Metallic gold fabric (for welting). 4″ x 28″
Poly-cotton (for inner backing). 12″ x 28″
Dark natural linen (for sides). 5″ x 28″
Uncovered welt filler. 60″
Metallic brocade (for ends). 7″ x 28″
1/2″ wide taupe decorative rope. 36″ (or 72″ for both ends)
Sewing and metallic thread
Fiberfill
Tools: zipper foot, 36″ metal ruler

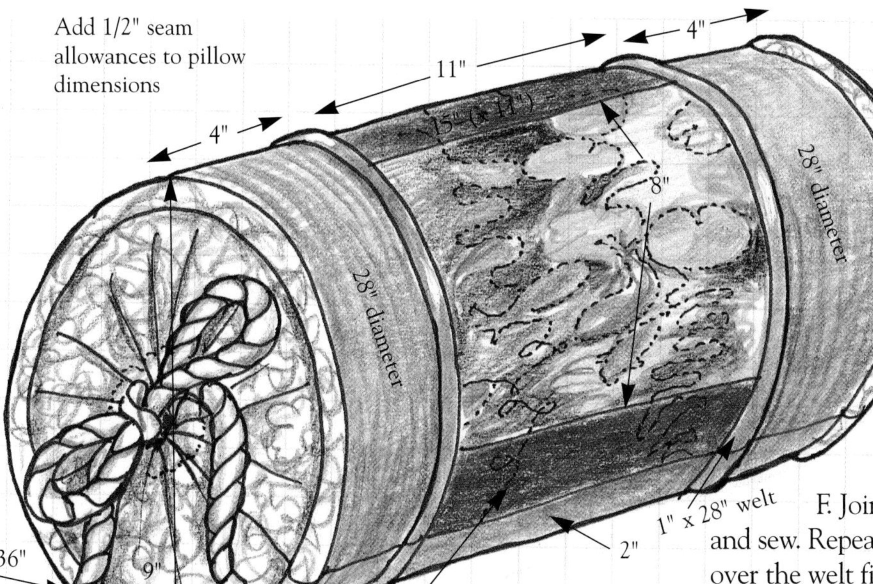

Making the pattern: Measure from the diagram and follow as in Project 47 (see page 118).

Transfer the photo image: See Project 47 (see page 117).

Sewing the pillow:

❶ Assemble center strip:

A. Join the 3″ peach strip to the 4″ purple, to the 8-1/2″ trimmed image, to the 16″ purple for a total of 28″ x 12″ (1/2″ seam allowances included).

B. Make a sandwich of inner backing, fiberfill stuffing, and assembled center, pin to anchor.

C. Free-motion stitch around various elements in the photo and continue onto the satin frame.

D. Add metallic welting.

E. Join the side pieces.

From here the pillow varies from Project 47 instructions.

F. Join the end to the side face-to-face, pin, and sew. Repeat. For welting, fold the end at the seam over the welt filler. Sew with a zipper foot on the seam line to make welting. Repeat.

G. For a tie casing: On the end turn a 1/4″ double hem in the side edge from both corners toward the center for 4″ and sew. Measure the end piece 4″ from welt. Fold under to make a 1-1/2″ casing.

H. Thread the rope or put it in the hem before hemming it. Wrap rope ends with matching thread and touch with Fraycheck to secure. Pull the rope as tightly as possible and tie in a bow. Repeat for the other end, or gather it, and sew closed.

Project 49:

Heron wall hanging

The Letchworth's home looks out over mangrove islands full of egrets' nests. This great blue heron visits our Florida home hoping for a snack. He seems to eat anything. Use the heron pattern, or see who's flying around your backyard waiting to model for you.

RIGHT: Just slide open the door wall and this great blue heron comes flapping across the water to wait for a handout... and pose for the wall hanging.

BELOW: This tall, skinny bird suits an oriental-style long, skinny wall hanging. The project hangs by a rod cord, then rolls up to store.

You need:

Bird:
Head. Black fabric 1-1/2˝ x 3˝
Face. White fabric 1-1/2˝ x 2˝
Neck. Gray fabric 3˝ x 6˝
Wing. "Feather" print fabric 5˝ x 11˝
Chest. Striped blue-gray fabric 3˝ x 8˝
Legs. Rusty coral fabric 4˝ x 7˝
Background: Eggshell poly-cotton 13˝ x 21˝ (need two)
Frame. Natural dark linen 19˝ x 32˝
Top End. Ecru mattelesse 19˝ x 12˝
Bottom End. Ecru mattelesse 19˝ x 13˝
Welting. Black poly-cotton 19˝ x 4˝
Back: Natural dark linen 19˝ x 48˝
HeatnBond fusible. 1 yard
Tear-away backing. 13˝ x 21˝
Black and gray machine embroidery threads
20˝ Dowels (need two)
Cord. 30˝
Tools: tracing paper, backing paper, chalk pencil, yardstick, sharp scissors, pins, iron, ironing board

Fabrics: The fabrics, chosen for their color, include a patch of my husband's tie, an upholstery scrap, and a quilting fabric. If you mix fabrics make sure they iron at similar temperatures and are of a similar weight for ease of handling.

Pattern: Photocopy or scale up. Trace a second copy on tracing paper. Make patterns for the image pieces, adding 1/8˝ seam allowances where they overlap. Measure and cut rectangular fabric by the diagram plus 1/2˝ seam allowances.

Sewing the object:

1 Background: Cut two backgrounds and fuse together with HeatnBond for stabilizing. You can see the pattern through both layers.

2 Image:
A. Cut out the copied image pieces.
B. Trace the pieces on HeatnBond's smooth side (the adhesive side is pebbly), but don't cut them out yet.
C. Iron the HeatnBond patterns on the fabric back. Cut out the image and peel the paper backing.
D. Lay the background over the pattern and pin it to the ironing board. Arrange the pieces on the background according to the pattern and iron one piece at a time. Trace detail lines with chalk pencil.
E. Pin tear-away stabilizing paper on the back of the entire image.
F. Satin-stitch with black embroidery thread to outline all pieces. Switch to gray thread for the water and feathers.
G. Remove backing paper.

3 Assembling the piece:
A. Fold a hem around the background and press. Align it on the frame, pin, and topstitch.
B. Fold the welting pieces in half lengthwise, align them to the frame, and baste or pin.
C. Lay the end pieces face-to-face with the background and welting and sew these seams. Open and press the welting toward the image.
D. Match the finished front with the back face-to-face and seam along the side edges and across the top. Turn and press.
E. Fold a 1/2˝ hem, then a 1-1/2˝ rod pocket in each ends, and topstitch. Saw the dowels to size, paint them black, and slide them in.
F. Staple or tie a cord to the top rod for hanging.

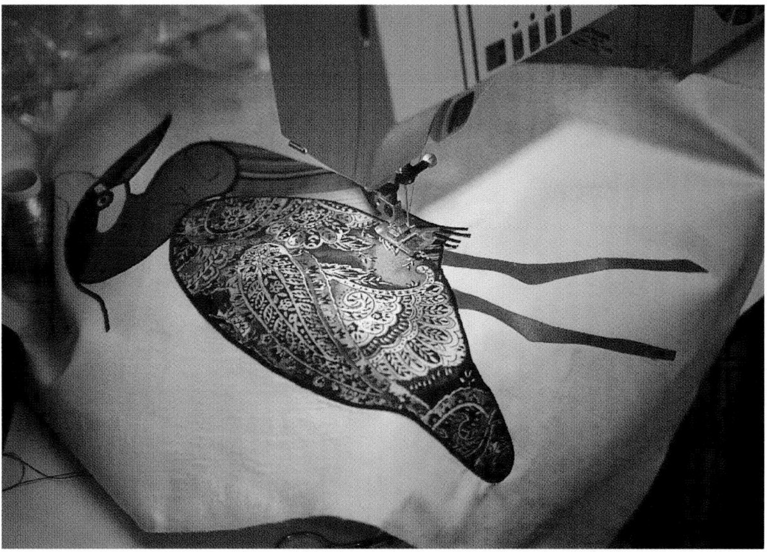

Selected fabrics simulating the heron's coloring are fused on a stabilized background and appliquéd with a satin-stitch outline.

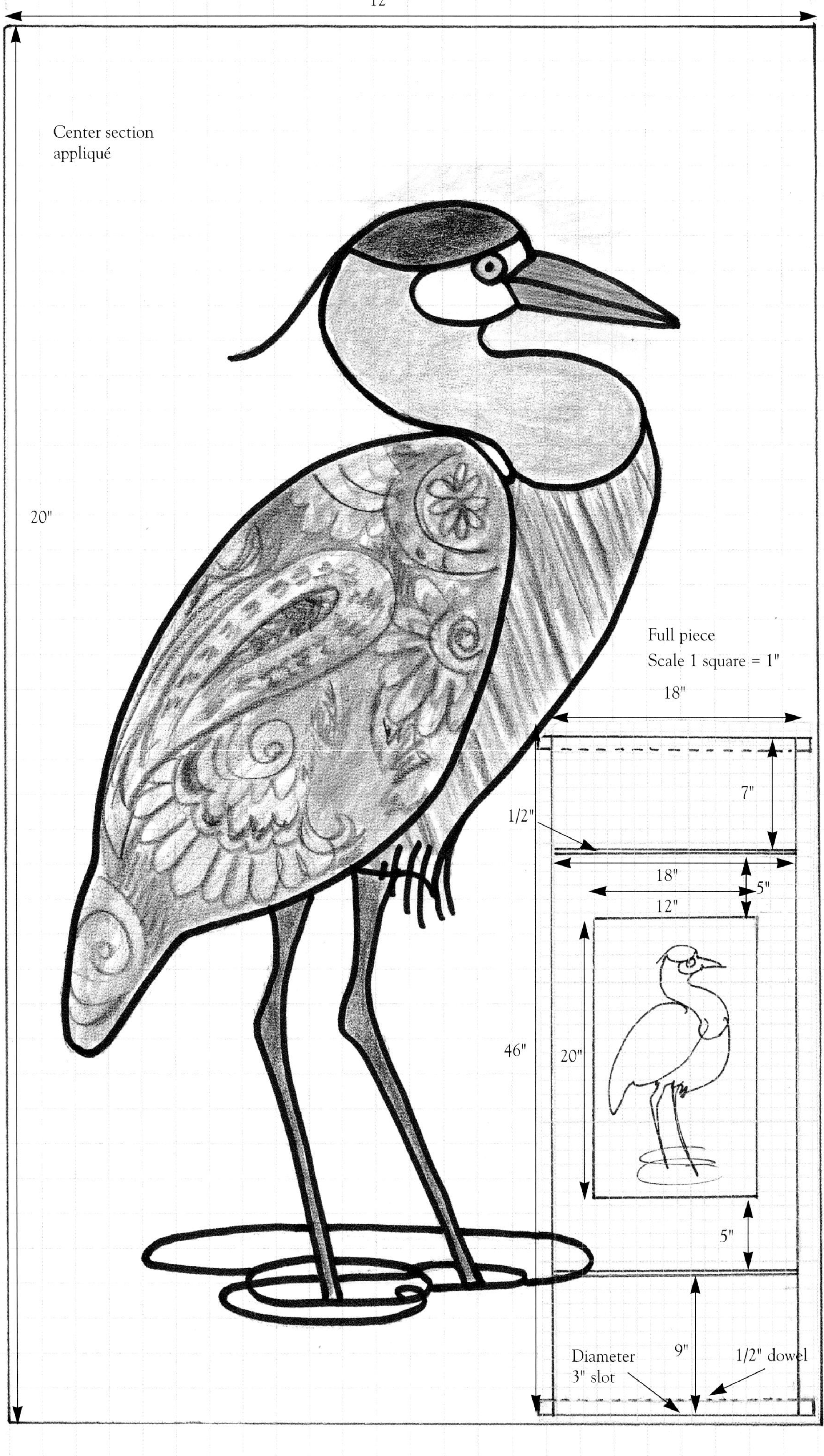

Scale 2 squares = 1"
12"
Center section
appliqué
20"
Full piece
Scale 1 square = 1"
18"
7"
1/2"
18"
5"
12"
46"
20"
5"
9"
Diameter
3" slot
1/2" dowel

Project 50: Tea cozy

The British keep their tea pots warm with an insulating cozy. Traditional Japanese nest the pot into an insulated fitted basket. This project is a combination of the two: a tea cozy Japanese style. It is modeled after the popular Japanese stone lanterns that appear in so many gardens both in Japan and around the world where oriental gardens are appreciated and used as models.

Inspiration for the tea cozy came from traditional Japanese stone lanterns, one shown here in Wallace Letchworth's well-tended garden. It fits Jane's tall tea pot perfectly. Photo by Jane Letchworth.

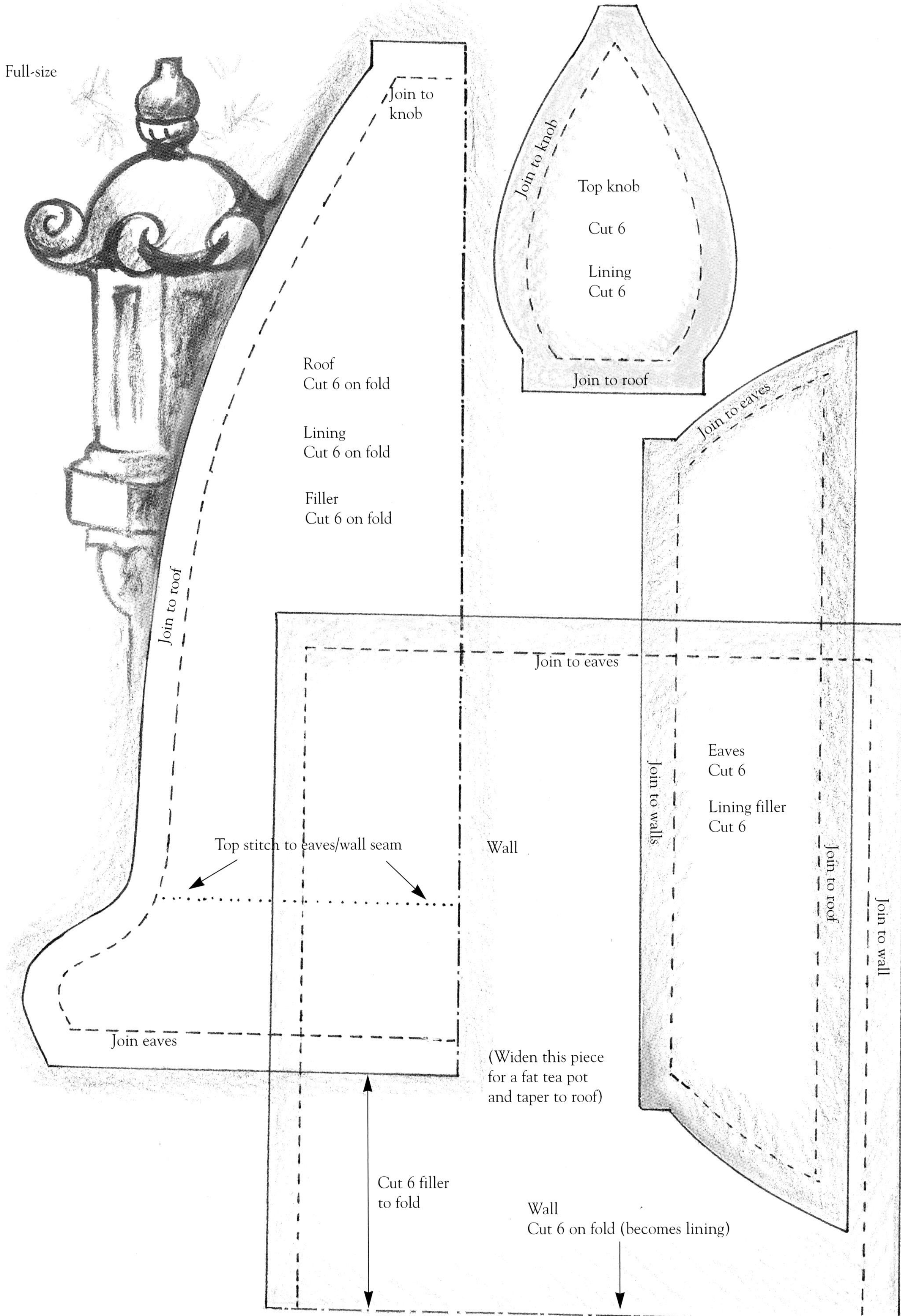
Full-size
Join to knob
Roof
Cut 6 on fold
Lining
Cut 6 on fold
Filler
Cut 6 on fold
Join to roof
Top stitch to eaves/wall seam
Join eaves
Top knob
Cut 6
Lining
Cut 6
Join to knob
Join to roof
Join to eaves
Eaves
Cut 6
Lining filler
Cut 6
Join to walls
Join to roof
Join to wall
Join to eaves
Wall
(Widen this piece
for a fat tea pot
and taper to roof)
Cut 6 filler
to fold
Wall
Cut 6 on fold (becomes lining)

You need:

Lantern exterior and lining (relate all of the fabrics to each other):
- *Textured taupe fabric. 12″ x 44″*
- *Navy/taupe striped poly-cotton. 9″ x 44″*
- *Brocade 14″ x 4″*

Pressed quilt batting (for filler). 21″ x 44″
Matching thread
Tools: scissors, quilting pins, pattern paper, chalk pencil

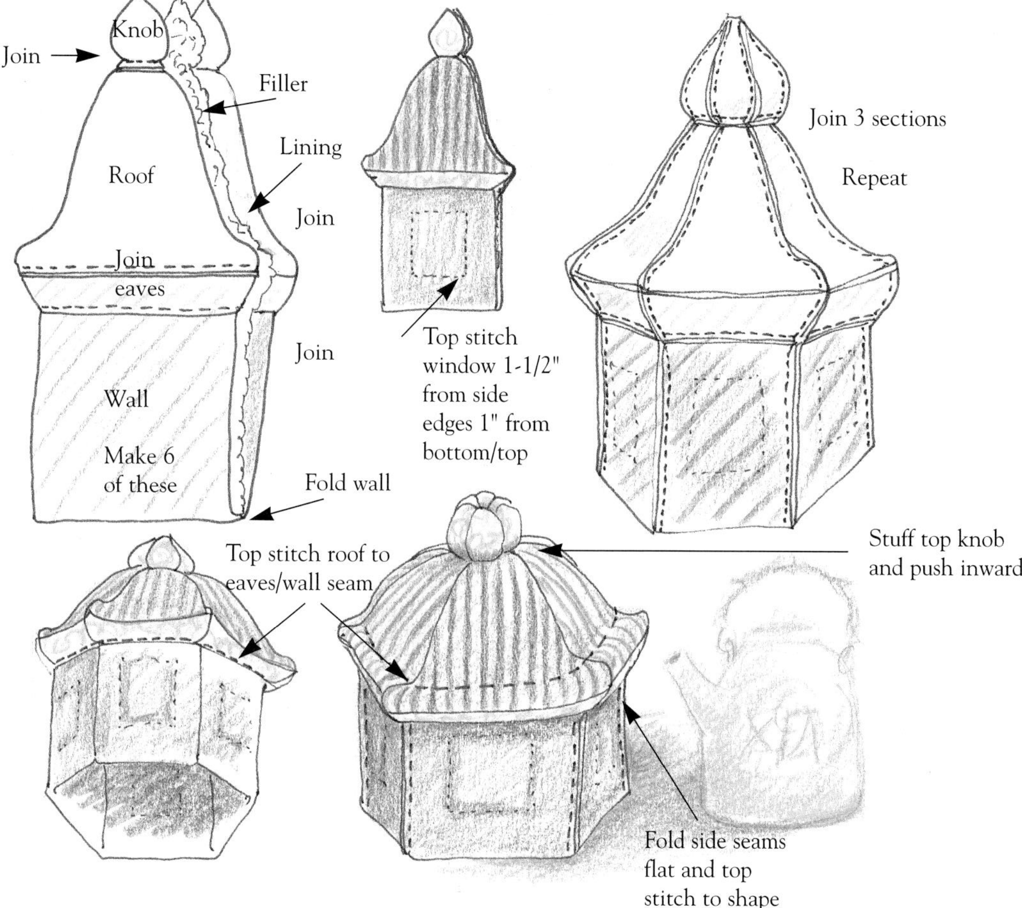

FABRICS: Fabrics selected suggest several Japanese elements: the stone of garden lanterns, the common blue-tiled roofs, and the glitter of gilded temples. This project is complicated and takes craftsmanship—but is fun when it turns out!

PATTERN: Trace or photocopy the pattern: top knob, eaves, roof, wall, lining, filler. Cut six of each piece. Mark the window shapes on the walls with chalk pencil.

Making the lantern cozy:

1. To assemble each side, stack each piece faceup, filler and lining. Align the top/filler/lining face-to-face to the roof/filler/lining. Next join the roof, etc., to the eaves, etc. Join the eaves to the wall. Align the wall face-to-face to the lining (no filler in this seam), stopping at the seam line and backstitching a stitch. Repeat for all six sides to complete six assembled strips.
2. Quilt the walls:
   A. Fold the lower half of the wall up over the filler to form the inside lining. Match the eaves seams and pin.
   B. Topstitch the window shapes.
3. Join the completed strips.
   A. Place two strips face-to-face, matching the edges, pin, and sew with 1/4″ seam allowance. Trim seam allowances to 3/16″ and clip inside curves at the roof

Mats and coasters absorb moisture and spills, cushion the dishes, and provide color and texture—and they are very easy to make. The metallic brocade shown is backed with natural linen with a thin layer of quilting filler. For the coasters you need a 5" circle of fabric each plus filler and backing. The mat measures 14" x 19" with the same filler and backing. Cut all three layers and serge the edges using a three-thread flat hem setting, or use an overcast stitch on your regular machine. To sew the coaster in a circle smoothly, press your left forefinger firmly in the center of the coaster and let the feed dogs pull the coaster in a circle. Use woolly nylon, a metallic, or colored thread for accent.

corners.

B. Join a third strip to make half the cozy. Repeat to assemble the other half.

C. Press open the roof seams and join one completed half to the other. Pin sides together and begin to stitch on the lining 1˝ before the eaves seam and sew all around the filled pieces. Continue sewing to an inch past the top of the lining. This will leave an opening to turn.

D. Trim all seam allowances at the eaves, turn, and press.

4 Shaping the lantern.

A. Fold the roof edge and eaves back-to-back. Pin from roof seam to eaves seam at the corners. Topstitch on the eaves/wall seam line around the roof. This forms the protruding roof edge. (See page 125)

B. Fold a wall corner outward, linings face-to-face. Topstitch this seam from the wall base to 1/2˝ from the eaves. This seam shapes the lantern as well as covers the lining's raw edges.

C. Push a ring of stuffing into the top and poke the center into the ring.

D. Hand stitch the lining closed.

Sources

BOOKS, CATALOGUES, AND MAIL-ORDER

BOOKS BY CAROLYN VOSBURG HALL:

Stitched and Stuffed Art, Doubleday
Soft Sculpture, Davis Publications
Sewing Machine Crafts Book, VanNostrand Reinhold
Teddy Bear Crafts Book, Prentice Hall
A to Z Soft Animals, Prentice Hall
Friendship Quilts, Chilton
Pictorial Quilts, Chilton
Alphabet Stitchery, Chilton

CHILTON/KRAUSE BOOKS ON RELATED CRAFTS

The Complete Book of Machine Embroidery, Robbie Fanning
Contemporary Quilting Techniques, Pat Caims
Fabric Lovers Handbook, Margaret Dittman
Speed-Cut Quilts, Donna Poster

OTHER BOOKS

Imagery on Fabric, Jean Ray Laury, C&T Publishing

CATALOGS AND SOURCES

Brewer Sewing Supplies Company
3800 West 42 Street
Chicago, IL 60632
(800) 444-3111
Wide range of sewing supplies; catalog available

Clotilde, Inc.
B3000
Louisiana, MO 63353
(800) 772-2891
Threads Books, notions, sewing machine feet; catalog available

Fairfield
P.O. Box 1 130
Danbury, CT 06813
(800) 243-0989
Stuffings of many kinds; catalog available

JoAnn Stores, Inc.
5555 Darrow Rd.
Hudson, OH 44236-4011
Wide range of fabrics and craft supplies; consult local phone directory for local outlets

Keepsake Quilting—the Quilter's Wishbook
Route 25B, P.O. Box 1618
Centre Harbor, NH 03226-1618
(800) 865-9458
Quilting fabrics and supplies, books, charming catalog available

Nancy's Notions
333 Beichl, P.O. Box 683
Beaver Dam, WI 53916-0683
(800) 833-0690
Threads, books, notions, photo transfer kits; catalog available

Sulky
3113-D Broadpoint Drive
Harbor Heights, FL 33983
(800) 874-4115
Elegant embroidery threads in metallic and rayons, machine embroidery supplies; catalog available

MAGAZINES ON SEWING

The Creative Machine
Open Chain Publishing
P.O. Box 2634-NL
Menlo Park, CA 92426
Robbie Fanning and her readers' advice on sewing

Fiberarts
50 College Street
Asheville, NC 28801-2896
Artist's fiber works, ads for supplies

Sew News
P.O. Box 1790
Peoria, IL 61656
Sewing techniques and ads for supplies and services

Threads
Taunton Press
63 S. Main Street
P.O. Box 506
Newtown, CT 06470-5506
Articles on sewing and fiberarts, ads for products, and supplies

Index